Truths About Whisky

John Jameson and Son

TRUTHS ABOUT WHISKY.

TRUTHS

ABOUT

WHISKY.

SECOND EDITION REVISED.

LONDON :

PRINTED BY SUTTON SHARPE AND CO.,

145, QUEEN VICTORIA STREET, E.C.

1879.

P

CONTENTS.

———

CHAPTER I.

CHAPTER VII.

CHAPTER VIII.

CHAPTER IX.

CHAPTER X.

LIST OF ILLUSTRATIONS.

TRUTHS ABOUT WHISKY.

CHAPTER I.

THE POSITION OF THE AUTHORS.

THE four firms of Whisky distillers by whom this book is published, Messrs. John Jameson and Son, Wm. Jameson and Co., John Power and Son, and George Roe and Co., who have for the last two years been engaged in an endeavour to place some check upon the practices of the fraudulent traders by whom silent spirit, variously disguised and flavoured, is sold under the name of Whisky, have come to the conclusion that their efforts in this direction are more likely to be successful if their own position with regard to the genuine manufacture is exactly known. Within the limits of the spirit trade, of course, this condition is already fulfilled; but it is important that it should also be fulfilled with regard to consumers and to the public. The fraudulent trade, although it could not exist without the complicity of great houses, yet exists mainly by the sufferance of the retail purchaser; for, if he were to insist upon being supplied with Whisky when he asks for it, and with silent spirit only when he asks for that, there would be an end of the element of deception which now enters so largely into the case. The authors cannot raise the smallest objection to the manufacture and sale of silent spirit, in whatever quantities

B

it may be required for the supply of any legitimate demand; either as an avowed substitute for Whisky for the use of those who like it, or for any one of an infinite number of possible applications in the arts. The point of their objection rests solely upon the substitution of silent spirit for Whisky when Whisky is demanded; and the validity of this objection must be admitted to depend upon the correctness of their definition of Whisky as a spirit which is distilled either from malt, or a mixture of malt and unmalted corn, from barley or oats, or malt, or from a mixture of them, in a so-called pot-still, which brings over, together with the spirit, a variety of flavouring and other ingredients from the grain. It is obvious that, if the grain were mouldy, or damaged, or for any reason ill-flavoured, the spirit thus made would be undrinkable; or, at least, would be of manifestly inferior quality; and hence the method of manufacture described requires, as an essential condition of its success, that only the very best grain and malt which can be procured should be employed. Silent spirit, on the contrary, is made in what are called "patent" stills from any vegetable matter which contains the materials necessary for fermentation; and the patent still, when it is properly and carefully managed, brings over alcohol and water only, leaving all flavouring matter behind. Hence, damaged grain or potatoes, molasses refuse, and various other waste products, are cast into the all-devouring maw of the patent still, and they all yield alcohol and water by distillation; so that, if alcohol and water were Whisky, they would all yield Whisky. As a matter of fact, these things no more yield Whisky than they yield wine or beer. Alcohol and water enter into the composition of all fermented drinks without exception; and these drinks are indebted for their severally distinctive qualities to the other things, over and above alcohol and water, which they respectively contain. In the case of Whisky, the distinctive characters are due to the grain products already mentioned; and these are not only sources of flavour, but also, when sufficiently matured by keeping, undergo development into a number of volatile ethers, so subtle that they almost elude chemical analysis, but which are easily discoverable by the nose and by the palate, and still more certainly by their power to produce exhilaration, which is altogether independent of the alcohol which holds them in solution. Fine Whisky, of good age, is so fragrant from the presence of these ethers that it might almost be used as a perfume; while silent spirit undergoes no change by keeping, and has only a peculiar penetrating odour of a kind which cannot be mistaken when it has once been perceived. In order to make silent spirit into a colourable imitation of Whisky—for it could not pass muster alone—it is drugged with different flavours, to which further reference will be made in the sequel.

Having said thus much by way of prelude to the general argument of the book, we come now to details about the position of the authors—details which are given for the sake of showing to what extent they are entitled to speak with authority upon the particular matter in hand.

With regard to the first of the firms in question, that of John Jameson and Son, its origin cannot now be traced. There is a tradition that it was founded by three gentlemen, one of whom was a baronet and another a retired general, but that they were unsuccessful in their enterprise and lost their capital. There is no one living who knows, and there is no discoverable documentary evidence to show, what was the date of foundation, neither can we even say at what date, prior to 1802, the distillery passed into the hands of the ancestor of the present proprietors. We only know that it has been in the possession of the same family for several generations, and that it has long been conspicuous, *primus inter pares*, for the unchallenged excellence of its products.

The second distillery, that of Messrs. Wm. Jameson and Co., has been in the possession of the family of the present proprietors since the year 1779. When purchased by their ancestor it was only a small undertaking; but from the superior quality of the Whisky which it produced, considerable enlargements soon became necessary. These enlargements were repeated from time to time; and, about eight years ago, the increasing demand for the Whisky rendered it necessary to increase the plant to the extent represented by an outlay of nearly £100,000. The yards and buildings now occupy a surface of ten acres of ground; and comprise corn stores, kilns, grinding mills, mash-house, spirit stores, cooperage, bonded warehouses, fermenting lofts, and other requirements for the conduct of the manufacture. The corn stores are capable of containing 30,000 barrels of sixteen stone each. The grinding mills can turn out 150 tons of ground corn in twenty-four hours. The mash-house, or brew-house, contains two tuns, which are the largest in the kingdom, being upwards of forty feet in diameter and ten feet deep, besides brewing vats and boiling coppers. In the fermenting lofts there are thirteen fermenting vessels or backs, some of which will contain 100,000 imperial gallons. The still-house is in proportion to the other arrangements, and contains four large pot-stills. In the spirit-house, the vat from which the Whisky is racked into casks keeps twenty men employed at a time. The bonded warehouses are nine in number will contain 20,000 hogsheads, and have been carefully constructed with a view to proper ventilation, and to the preservation of the spirit under circumstances favourable to its being matured. The present cooperage was only completed about five years ago, end covers an acre of ground, where there is every modern appliance for cleansing and purifying casks. The water supply, of which there will be more to say hereafter, is mainly derived from the river Poddle, which flows through the distillery.

The firm of John Power and Son, John's Lane Distillery, Dublin, was established in 1791, by Mr. James Power, the great-grandfather of the present proprietors, and during the last few years the whole distillery has been rebuilt upon an improved plan, and fitted with new plant. The works now cover five acres of ground, and contain appliances similar to those of the distillery last described. The storehouse for raw or unmalted corn is 153 ft. in length by 95 ft. in breadth. It is five stories high, and is capable of containing 3,000 tons of grain. The grain is delivered in two receiving rooms on the ground floor, from whence it is conveyed to the lofts by elevators, and is then distributed by archimedean screws. The mill contains four pairs of stones, driven by a steam engine of one hundred and sixty nominal horse power, and is capable of grinding upwards of sixty tons every twenty-four hours. The barley for malting is received into separate lofts, where it is distributed for the subsequent processes in the same manner as the raw barley; and the meal is conveyed by elevators to a store over the brewhouse, whence it is discharged into large mash tuns beneath, each of which is sufficiently capacious to mash thirty-five tons daily.

The still-house contains four pot-stills of large capacity, together with five receivers and three chargers. The Whisky produced by these stills is pumped from the testing room to the spirit store, where it is put into large vats, and reduced to an uniform strength of twenty-five per cent. overproof before it is filled into casks. The bonded warehouses are seventeen in number, and afford storage-room for two years' manufacture.

The fourth, or Thomas Street Distillery, that of George Roe and Co., was founded before the middle of the eighteenth century, and became the property of an ancestor of the present proprietor, Mr. Henry Roe, junior, in the year 1775. Originally of small dimensions, the works have been extended in various times during the last eighty years, and within the last ten years very large sums of money have been expended upon them. Four additional stills were built in 1872; and these, with other plant erected shortly afterwards, have almost doubled the producing power of the concern, which is now the largest pot-still distillery in the United Kingdom. During the course of 1877, large corn stores and a new drying kiln were added; and with this increased power about 5000 barrels of barley and oats are dried every week. The corn-mill contains seven pairs of stones, and can grind 1500 barrels of corn in twenty-four hours. There are three mash tuns, the largest of which is 36 ft. in diameter and 7 ft. 6 in. in depth, and eight large pot-stills of the usual construction.

For very many years before steam power was introduced, the machinery of this distillery was driven by
wind; and the windmill employed for the purpose,
which is upwards of 120 ft. in height, still remains, and
is surmounted by a copper dome, on which stands a
large iron figure of St. Patrick. The windmill has,
however, been superseded by steam engines, the three
largest of which work up to 120, 150, and 180 horse-
power respectively. Besides these, there are several
smaller engines, used for driving pumps and for other
minor work. The chargers, receivers, worm-tubs, and
other necessary utensils, are all on a scale of magnitude
corresponding with the rest of the plant; and the
Whisky is stored in warehouses, of which there are
seventeen, several of them capable of containing 12,000
casks each. Plans for large additions are at present
under consideration, and a great extension of the works
cannot be long delayed.

It will be observed, in the foregoing enumeration
of some of the chief points of the four distilleries, that
no mention has been made of patent stills; and the four
establishments are all alike in this respect, that no patent
still exists among them. They make, and they can
make, nothing but pot-still spirit; that is to say, real
genuine Whisky, and they have no means, appliances,
or opportunity, for mixing this with any inferior liquid
before it is sent out to their respective customers.

Besides those of the Authors, there are perhaps,
fourteen other distilleries in various parts of Ireland,
in which nothing but pot-still Whisky is made. Those
situated in the provinces are mostly on a small
scale, and it may fairly be said that they bear
to the great Dublin firms the sort of relation which
is borne in England by the ale and beer brewers

of small market towns to the Breweries of London or of Burton-upon-Trent. The provincial pot-still Whisky is a genuine article, fairly entitled to be called Whisky; but the Dublin houses, by their long-established position and their large capital, not only command the grain market, and can secure for themselves the pick of each years' harvest, but they also command the best manufacturing skill which money and experience can procure.

While such, for many years, has been the Authors' position of supremacy as manufacturers, the conditions of the Whisky Trade have nevertheless been such as to keep their names, to a very great extent, concealed from the knowledge of consumers. It has been the practice of the four firms for many years, not merely to sell chiefly to large dealers, but to sell without taking precautions for the preservation of the purity and simplicity of their products; and out of this practice sundry complications ultimately arose. Certain of these dealers began to push their own trade with public-houses and private consumers by means of costly and continued advertisements; and in this way the position in the estimation of the public which should have been held by the best manufacturers was gradually usurped by the dealers; while, in course of time, some of the dealers, finding that they had established a market for their own wares, began to seek how they might turn this market to the largest pecuniary account, by increasing their profits upon the Whisky. They were not content with the honest profit which they derived as middlemen, but sought to increase this profit even at the cost of having recourse to means which rendered it no longer honest. The first step in this direction was to adulterate the Whisky of the Dublin makers with provincial Whisky of a cheaper and coarser character, and to sell the whole mixture at the price of the more costly of the two varieties of spirit which entered into its composition. At first, this was done somewhat bashfully, and under the pretext that these dealers, by dint of great knowledge and experience, had found out how to mix two or more varieties of Whisky in such manner as to produce a result better than any of its component parts. The process was delicately called "blending" and, although it would seem that nothing more than a faint gleam of common sense was required in order to show the character of the proceeding, it is said that there are people still living who seriously believe that to mix good and bad Whisky together is a desirable proceeding in the interests of the consumer. The first "blenders" were enabled, to some small extent, to undersell those of their rivals who had not yet discovered or practised the art; but in trade such practices soon become known to those whose business it is to find them out, and blending became almost universal. In the meanwhile, the increasing employment of the patent still had brought copious supplies of silent spirit into the market; and the blenders soon availed themselves of these supplies as sources of additional cheapness. They were no longer content to dilute the genuine Dublin with the coarse provincial Whisky; but they afterwards diluted the mixture with silent spirit, and they selected the coarsest and strongest tasted provincial Whisky they could find, in order to give flavour to the otherwise insipid compound. By-and-bye, the Dublin Whisky was first diminished in quantity, and ultimately was even suffered to drop out altogether, and in course of time the provincial Whisky followed the Dublin. Pressure was next brought to bear upon the revenue authorities to permit the "Blending" of "Plain British Spirit" in bond; and dealers were allowed to bring silent spirit from any part of the United Kingdom to any other part, and to mix it with any other spirit, being of British manufacture, in any proportions which seemed good to them. Great manufactories of silent spirit existed in Scotland; but Irish Whisky was held in more general esteem than Scotch, and so the Scotch and English silent spirit was sent to Dublin, to be returned from thence to England as Dublin or Irish Whisky. Thousands of gallons of silent spirit were sent from Glasgow or from Liverpool to Dublin or to Belfast; and, having been mixed in bond with other spirit like itself, from the same or from other sources, and perhaps with a little, say 10 per cent., of genuine coarse Whisky, the compound was reshipped immediately from the Irish port, with a Belfast or a Dublin Custom-House permit, as Dublin or Irish Whisky, was sold under this name in England, and was sent from England to all other parts of the world. The active competition among dealers to undersell one another drove them continually to lower and lower shifts, until at length even the modicum of coarse Whisky was omitted from the mixture, and an attempt was made to give an approach to the flavour of Whisky by chemical means alone. The great Dublin houses were in time brought face to face with a very serious state of things. The manufacture which their firms had introduced, and which had become famous, was being gradually superseded by a fraudulent admixture of less than half the value, which was retailed at a lower price than that at which genuine Whisky could be sold to the wholesale dealer, or even produced at the distillery. The imitation was so wanting in all the essentials of

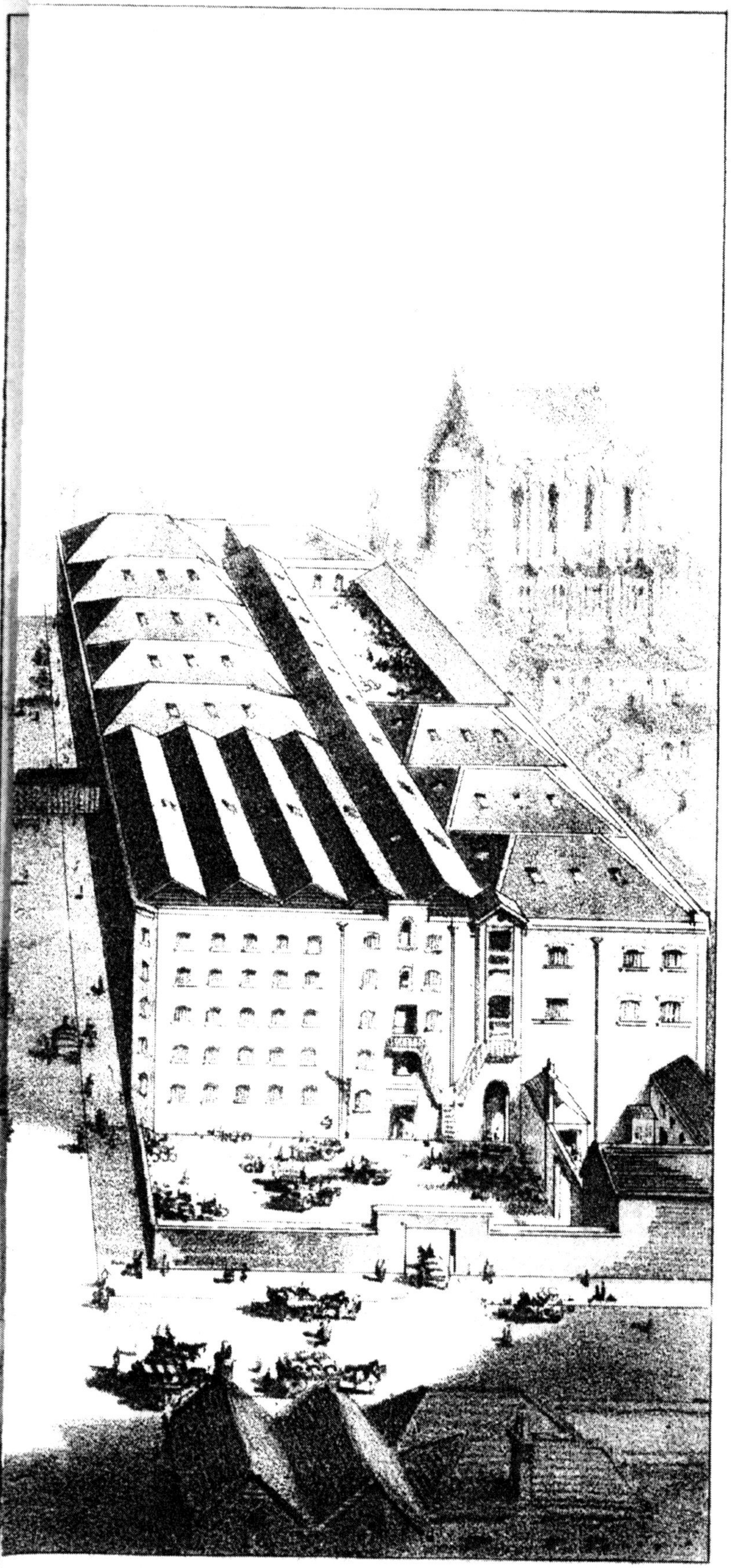

DUBLIN

real Whisky that it had no other value than as a mere stimulant for dram-drinkers, possessing none of the dietetic qualities of genuine Whisky; and the consumer, who had no means of getting Whisky at all, would soon have ceased to know even what it ought to be, so that the genuine spirit would have been displaced and driven out of the field by the fictitious. The make of the great firms seldom reached the public in its purity, but only as a flavouring ingredient in some few of the best of the spurious kinds; and even in these the importance and meaning of this flavour were gradually ceasing to be recognised. Some of the dealers, who had at first been content to import their silent spirit from England or Scotland, at last began to find that they could make it themselves; and a vastly increased number of patent stills invaded even the soil of Ireland. In Belfast, Cork, Dundalk, Limerick, and Londonderry patent stills were established, sometimes with, and sometimes without, pot-stills in the same distillery; and silent spirit, always under the name of Whisky, became an extensive Irish manufacture. In these circumstances the authors had only two courses open to them. It is much more costly to produce Whisky than to produce silent spirit; and, as long as both were supposed to be essentially the same liquid, and were in competition with one another, the silent spirit lowered the price of Whisky until the latter could scarcely be sold at a price to pay for its manufacture. The Dublin firms might have thrown down their pot-stills, replaced them by patent ones, and have gone into the silent spirit or fictitious Whisky trade with an amount of capital, and with other advantages, which would have enabled them to defy the competition of smaller and newer establishments. Instead of doing this, they determined to accept the only possible alternative, and to appeal to the public in defence of the purity and excellence of their manufacture. They determined to come out from behind the veil of middlemen by which they had too long been concealed from the consumer, and to declare the true nature of the stuff which was being sold as Whisky and of the imposition which was being practised upon the public. They do not in the least degree desire to interfere with the manufacture of silent spirit; but they do wish to interfere with its being sold under the name of Whisky. They had scarcely arrived at the determination to take some joint action in the matter, when the *Times* paper devoted an article to the subject, in which the fraudulent character of the so-called Whisky trade was briefly, but forcibly, described, in terms the precise accuracy of which has not been, and cannot be, impugned. Other newspapers, notably the *Daily Telegraph*, *Punch*, and the *Medical Examiner*, followed the lead of the *Times* upon the question; and the authors of this volume, as their first step in the campaign upon which they had determined to enter, caused copies of the newspaper articles, with a connecting thread of narrative, to be printed in pamphlet form and widely circulated. The effect of this publication soon became apparent. Consumers began to learn what Whisky was, and what it ought to be; and to distinguish it from silent spirit, however cunningly flavoured. The public began to take the matter into their own hands, and to insist upon being supplied with what they asked for. The true nature of blending was rendered manifest to the humblest capacity; and the practice was reduced from the level of a fine art to that of a vulgar fraud. Members of the House of Commons began to take interest in the question; and some awkward inquiries were made of Ministers with regard to the facilities for fraud which were afforded by the Customs Regulations. There was abundant evidence that the Authors had not over-estimated either the strength of their position or the righteousness of their cause; and they have been encouraged to persist in their endeavour to spread abroad a knowledge of the nature of Whisky and of its counterfeits, as well as of the conditions under which the trade in counterfeit Whisky has arisen and has been carried on. In such an endeavour, it is an essential condition of success to act upon the well-known principle of the late President Lincoln, and to keep on "pegging away." The first pamphlet has done its work; and these pages, which contain a more general and more extended view of the whole subject, have been written in order to replace it.

CHAPTER II.

THE QUALITIES AND POPULARITY OF GENUINE DUBLIN WHISKY.

DR. JOHNSON defines Whisky to be a corruption of Usquebaugh, an Irish and Erse word, which signifies the water of life. He adds that the Irish sort is particularly distinguished for its pleasant and mild flavour, but that the Highland sort is somewhat hotter; and he explains this in a way which, if it was ever correct, has long ceased to be so. He says that the Irish sort is drawn, *i.e.*, distilled, from aromatics; meaning, we presume, that aromatic substances were added to the mash of grain, in order to give a pleasant flavour to the result. He therefore bears testimony to the correctness of our argument, that genuine Whisky derives a flavour from the substances from which it is distilled, and it is plain that patent still or silent spirit, which is not thus flavoured, cannot fulfil the terms of the definition, and is not Whisky. In Dr. Johnson's time, however, and for long after, the manufacture of Irish Whisky was carried on in a very primitive fashion, and the bulk of the spirit was drunk when quite new, partly from want of knowledge of the good effects of keeping it, partly from want of storage conveniences, and sometimes to conceal the precious brew from the prying eyes of the Collectors of Revenue. We are merely hazarding a conjecture, but it seems more than probable that the first "Old" Irish Whisky became so from being buried in haste for the purpose of concealment, and perhaps not disinterred until after the lapse of years. Unless in such circumstances as these, we fancy Whisky would always have kept badly among our countrymen, who, like the Scotchman lately made famous in *Punch,* would not be likely to sleep well when there was any quantity of the precious liquid in the house. However this may be, and whether or not we do our countrymen an unintentional injustice in the supposition, there is evidence that the manufacture more than a century ago had become established in Dublin, and in the hands of the ancestors of the Authors; who, there can be no doubt, would soon discover that the addition of the aromatics was unnecessary, if the spirit could be kept long enough to acquire the peculiar and inimitable fragrance which is given to it by age, and by age alone. In order fully to explain this fragrance, it would be needful to enter into chemical details of a kind which would have little interest for readers who are not already conversant with them; but the general facts may be briefly expressed The pot-still, as already stated, does not yield a product containing merely alcohol and water, but one which also contains, in intimate mixture, or in solution, many other matters which are yielded by the grain, either as *educts,* matters which naturally exist and are simply taken out, or as *products,* matters which are themselves the results of chemical changes in the grain elements during the process of fermentation and distillation. These substances are present in new pot-still Whisky, chiefly in the form of volatile oils and vegetable acids, and their quantity, as well as their precise characters, will depend greatly upon the quality of the grain, upon the way in which it has been treated prior to distillation, and upon the skill and care with which the distillation has been conducted. Between wine and Whisky there is a close parallelism; for in both the new liquid is comparatively unpleasant, and in both it contains materials which shape themselves, if the opportunity is afforded them, into fresh compounds which are highly and deservedly esteemed. These materials are, as said above, chiefly vegetable acids and volatile oils; and the mutual reactions which occur between them and the alcohol, lead to the gradual formation of various ethers of great fragrance. It is well known that alcohol, when but little diluted, restrains organic change; and hence, as a general rule, the greater the alcoholic strength of any liquid, the more slowly will it undergo the changes which constitute maturation. A pure wine of high class, say a fine vintage Burgundy, undergoes maturation comparatively speedily; and, after having been only three or four years in bottle, it fills the room with perfume as soon as the cork is drawn. Wine of equally good original quality, when brandied for the English market or to protect it during a voyage, will undergo maturation more slowly and better when in greater bulk; whence the long time required to bring some samples of Port to perfection, and whence, also, the love of connoisseurs for magnums. The finest Dublin Whisky, when made, is reduced to a uniform strength of twenty-five per cent. overproof; and is stored in casks of considerable size. Its great alcoholic strength causes it to undergo change only tardily; so that its full maturity and highest excellence cannot be reckoned upon under an age of from three to five years in the wood. The grain constituents of perfectly new

Whisky are not palatable in the estimation of people in general; but after about a year the Whisky may be said to be drinkable, after about two years to be good, and after about three years to be as good as anything with which the average consumer is likely to become acquainted. Those, however, who have only drunk three-year-old Whisky, can scarcely form an idea of the effect of longer keeping, always in the wood. The spirit is too strong, the preservative effect of its alcohol is too decided, for any beneficial change to occur in a small bulk hermetically sealed in a bottle, and maturation only becomes complete in large bulk and in wood, which permits the loss by evaporation of much of the original spirit. In order to arrive at perfection, it may be laid down as a general rule that Whisky stored at twenty-five per cent. over-proof should be left in the cask until its strength has fallen considerably; it may then be bottled, and preserved for an indefinite time without further change. When a bottle of such Whisky is opened, it literally, like fine old Burgundy, fills the room with its fragrance, and that fragrance is more delicate than anyone who is unacquainted with it, or who is acquainted only with the smell of common so-called Whisky, could by any possibility conceive. The fragrance is an evidence that all the grain products additional to the alcohol have undergone decomposition, and that their elements have been re-arranged into fresh combinations of a kind analogous to the vinous ethers, and which, like these, are among the most exhilarating of all stimulants. The stimulating characters of new wine, or of new Whisky, are due only to the quantity of alcohol which each contains, and may, therefore, be ascertained by the balance and the test-tube. But the stimulating characters of old wine

C

or of old Whisky are due also, and probably, in much
larger measure, to these ethers, which, like nearly all
the bodies of their class, are known to sustain the action
of the heart and pleasantly to excite the mental facul-
ties, without producing the subsequent depression
which so often attends upon the use of alcohol alone.
Unlike the alcohol, the ethers are not measurable.
They are extremely volatile, as is fully shown by the
prompt diffusion of their perfume; and they are also, in
chemical language, so unstable that they can neither
be fixed nor analysed. They all consist of the same
elements, and so far, when examined by ultimate
analysis, or resolution into their ultimate component parts,
they are all pretty nearly alike. Their different properties depend upon minute differences in the proportions
of these ultimate elements, or even in the molecular
arrangement by which they are combined, and these
differences defy analysis, although the results of each
arrangement may produce a different impression upon
the human senses, and a different effect upon the human
frame. Chemically speaking, a stench and a perfume, a
poison and a remedy, are often separated from each
other by curiously fine distinctions, or by differences of
which we should never conjecture the importance, if
this importance was not constantly made manifest to us
by difference of effect. The ethers of which we have
spoken all belong to what may be called the fusel-oil
family; and, in some varieties of spirit, fusel-oil is among
the forms in which they first appear. A Whisky containing an excess of fusel-oil is said to produce a peculiarly violent and dangerous form of inebriation, and such
an excess is only produced either by badly-conducted
distillation or by the use of improper materials. These
ethers, or certainly the common and at first unpalatable

grain products, may be likened to those qualities in youth which sometimes, especially if not wisely guided, display themselves by the process known as "sowing wild oats," but which, when a certain amount of irregular or untrained energy has been expended, form the basis of some of the noblest and most useful characters. Without the grain products the spirit would be alcohol and water, and nothing more, with no power of development and no capacity for improvement. With them, always supposing that they are yielded by good and well-managed grain, the capacities of improvement are infinite; and the Whisky, which when new is unpalatable, may yet, when it is old, more than maintain the best traditions of the family from which it springs.

In the days of our forefathers, when it was customary to drink solemnly to what were then called "sentiments," one of the most popular of these was the expression of a hope that the evening's pleasure might bear the morning's reflection. It is, perhaps, one of the most striking qualities of genuine and mature Dublin Whisky that it will bear this crucial test. The carefully-brewed glass of toddy, which enlivens talk and quickens fancy when friends are met together round the fireside, leaves no manner of sting behind. It conduces to quiet and dreamless slumber, and it allows the sleeper to wake refreshed, with a cool palate and an easy head, fit for the duties or the pleasures of the coming day. We once met at a dinner-party a wine merchant of great experience, whose opinion was asked about one of the vintages which graced the board. He replied, "I will tell you all I think about it in the morning." We believe that, especially for the unskilled in spirits, there is no better test than this.

Connoisseurs will tell, with a near approach to certainty, the qualities of a real or pretended Whisky by taste and odour, and especially by taste and odour after dilution with cold water; but for those who are not connoisseurs the best test is the state of the head and of the mouth next morning, when the spirit in question has been taken over night. We mean, of course, when it has been taken in moderation, for alcoholic excess, however good the alcohol, is always and to everyone injurious; if not at once, at least ultimately. We claim, however, for genuine Whisky, that it is the most wholesome form in which alcohol can be consumed, and that the ethers which it contains materially assist the alcohol in its beneficial action upon the organism. Unlike some wines, Whisky has no tendency to produce acid indigestion, and it is therefore especially suited to those who inherit, or who have developed for themselves, a gouty constitution. The experience of sportsmen proves it to be the best stimulant during long periods of exertion, when exposed to wet and cold in pedestrian excursions, in deer-stalking, shooting, fishing, or other forms of sport. As applied to these uses, there can be no doubt that the grain ethers play a most important part, acting, to a great extent, as better substitutes for alcohol, and rendering a smaller dose efficacious for the purposes required. We are committed, as a matter of course, to an entire dissent from the doctrines of those fanatical teetotalers who hold that alcohol, in whatever quantity, is always and everywhere injurious, and we cannot be expected to engage in any argument with them; but we must, nevertheless, express our surprise, assuming that they desire to make converts among reasonable and reasoning men, that they should have so completely left out of account, in the various experi-

ments which some of their body profess to have conducted, the way in which the action of alcohol may be
modified by the various substances with which it may
be combined. We read, for example, of experiments
made with "brandy;" but what is brandy? If the experiments had been made with something which was
called Whisky, it would have been highly important to
discover whether the liquid used was really Whisky
containing ethers in solution, or silent spirit consisting
only of alcohol and water. We must remember that
the ethers of wine are so potent that, if separated and
inhaled, they soon produce a complete insensibility,
during the continuance of which a surgical operation
may be performed without the knowledge of the person
who has inhaled them. Surely it is absurd to suppose
that an agent so powerful as this can exert no influence
when it is swallowed, or that it can be left wholly out
of account in estimating the qualities of any liquid which
contains it. We maintain that the presence of the grain
ethers is the *rationale* of the peculiar qualities of fine
Whisky, which is indebted to these ethers for a power
of stimulation far in excess of its alcoholic strength, as
well as for a wholesomeness greater than that of any
other accessible form of spirit, and for a popularity
which is the natural result and outcome of its qualities.
As hypocrisy is the homage which vice pays to virtue,
so the pains which have been taken to call silent spirit
by the name of Whisky, and not only by the name of
Whisky, but by the name of Irish or even specially of
Dublin Whisky, is a better tribute to the extent of its
popularity than all which we could urge on its behalf.
For several years past it has been worth the while of
certain dealers to incur the expense of conveying
millions of gallons of Scotch and English silent spirit to

Ireland, and generally either to Dublin or to Belfast, only in order to bring it back again under cover of a Dublin or Belfast permit, so that it might be falsely palmed off upon purchasers as of Dublin or Irish manufacture. In many instances the spirit has been returned on the same day as that on which it was landed in Ireland, and in the same casks; and it gained in selling price, by bearing an Irish permit, more than the cost of the freight both ways across St. George's Channel. Of late years, since silent spirit has been largely made in Ireland, so that the supplies for so-called blending purposes, that is to say, for reducing coarse provincial Whisky by means of silent spirit, have been to a great extent of home manufacture, not indeed Irish Whisky, but truly Irish spirit—the chief aim of importers has been to obtain the Dublin or the Irish permit, by which their foreign rubbish was palmed off upon the purchaser as Irish Whisky too. The unchecked continuance of recent practices would, undoubtedly, in a few years, lead the public to the apparent or supposed discovery that the good qualities of Irish or of Dublin Whisky had no better basis than the fond imaginations of a former generation of men ; and the Authors will have fulfilled the task which they have undertaken if they show, as they must unless their demonstration should fail to do justice to the facts of the case, that real Dublin Whisky is still as excellent a commodity as at any former time and that it still possesses all the high qualities for which it was prized and consumed by our forefathers. The *Times* newspaper, in commenting upon the adulteration of seeds, in a leading article published on the 4th of December, 1877, points out, with too much truth, that consumers are generally the last to care what they are paying for; but, in the present day, it is only by so caring that they can have any hope of escaping from the great and growing evil of fraudulent adulteration or substitution. It is one of the objects of this book besides explaining what the qualities of Dublin Whisky are, and how they are secured, to point out also in what way the purchaser may guard himself against being, deceived, and may render himself certain of obtaining Whisky when he asks for it and pays for it. In order to afford the public this protection, we must, as a *sine quâ non*, obtain their own intelligent co-operation; and we have the satisfaction of knowing that the tricks practised in the Whisky trade are so transparent that nobody who has once been told of them need ever again be deceived, if he will only take the trouble to be upon his guard. In this matter, as in so many others, a rogue is only a fool with a circumbendibus; and the traders who, for the sake of a brief time of profit, have been bent upon destroying one of the national industries of Ireland by the substitution of an inferior article for the time-honoured product, are very transparent in their ways. Like the fabled ostrich, they think themselves secure from detection as long as they can conceal the head of their offending; but they forget that this security lasts only so long as no hunter is in pursuit of them. We have made it our deliberate business to expose their devices, and we shall not leave any means untried by which an object in every way so desirable may be attained.

CHAPTER III.

PECULIARITIES OF THE DUBLIN MANUFACTURE: THE WATER SUPPLY.

WE have already stated, or have allowed it to be inferred, that the Whisky manufactured in Dublin by the well-tried plan of pot-still distillation, and of maturation by age alone, is superior to any that is made, even upon the same method, at any of the provincial distilleries; and we have explained this by reference to the advantages enjoyed by the Dublin houses in their great command of capital, of experience, and of skill, and also in the vastness of the scale upon which their operations are conducted. Their experience, in each case, is not only that of a single lifetime or generation, but it is tempered by the traditions handed down from generations which have passed away; and we constantly find that such empirical knowledge is in advance of the scientific or theoretical knowledge which is contemporaneous with it, and which often finds its best occupation in explaining the grounds of the truths which experience has already discovered to be true. Especially in the conduct of fermentation does this knowledge, based upon experience, come into constant use and application; and there are certain signs, as slight and indescribable, perhaps, as those which appeal to the proverbial weather wisdom of shepherds, which warn the old hand when it is time for him to intervene.

Signs of equal importance, and, it will be claimed, of even more precision, may be obtained by the application of scientific tests; but the mental perception of the experienced man is instantaneous, while the tests take time, and allow the best moment for action to pass away. Again, the Dublin houses, being practically exempt from the destructive competition downward in respect of price, which involves the spoiling of so many ships for the sake of saving a half-pennyworth of tar, are always in a position to buy the very best grain which is for sale, without allowing any other consideration than that of quality to interfere with them for a moment. The price of materials, and the quantity of product, are with them only secondary considerations; the first consideration being always and simply to make the best Whisky which it is possible for capital and skill to produce. Besides the powerful operation of these artificial causes, the Dublin manufacture is much indebted to a natural one, namely, to the character of the local water supply. It is well known that many great breweries are placed in a similarly advantageous position; that the water of the famous Southwark well has been largely contributory to the reputation which enabled Dr. Johnson, in his well-known advertisement of the business, to say that it implied a potentiality of wealth beyond the dreams of avarice; that some of the other London brewers are similarly favoured; that the water of Burton-upon-Trent forms part, at least, of the secret of the excellence of its ale, and that, to take an illustration from nearer home, the water of Dublin is the source of the stout which has made the name of Guinness a household word wherever there are civilised men who experience the sensation of thirst. All these various kinds of water have special powers of dissolving vegetable matters and of retaining vegetable aromas; and the water which is so excellent for stout is equally available for extracting the virtues of malt or grain in order to present them to the consumer in the form of Whisky. It is a very curious experiment to bring some Dublin water to London, and to make two infusions of tea, alike in all respects, save that one is made with the imported and the other with the London water. The former will be found to yield at once a more fully flavoured and a more deeply coloured infusion, showing that the Dublin water is a more powerful solvent than that of London. An analysis by Professor Wanklyn has shown that the water of the Canal which is used by us is alkaline to an extent which equals the presence of a pound and a half of carbonate of soda in 1000 gallons. The alkalinity in question is derived, of course, from filtration through the earth; and it is a curious though familiar fact that the natural medication of water by this process of earth filtration cannot be imitated by art. Chemists make the most precise analyses of medicinal mineral waters, and these are then imitated by laboratory processes until no tests could distinguish the original from the imitation—no test, that is, save one, the test which is applied by the human system when the water is taken as a remedy. No artificial substitute or imitation, even although to all appearance the same thing, ever fully equals the effect of the original; and it is the more necessary to lay stress upon this established lesson of experience, lest some maker of bad Whisky should try to improve his results, and to imitate Dublin water by adding to that which he employs a modicum of soda. We should explain also that the actual alkalinity, although estimated in terms of soda, does not consist entirely of that substance, but also of lime and of magnesia; so that an exact imitation is less than ever practicable In other respects the water is of average drinking purity, and presents no discoverable peculiarities It does not from this follow that it may possess none; for our faith in the growing science of chemistry is not sufficiently profound to induce us to place entire and absolute reliance upon all of its positive, and still less, therefore, upon all of its negative results. Because things are not discovered, it does not follow that they may not be there; and we speak of the special value of Dublin water for Whisky making, from the results of long experience, as a fact about which there can be no question, and which may or may not be adequately explained by the alkalinity which we have mentioned. We contend only for the fact, and for its importance in pointing to Dublin as the natural home of the manufacture; and we leave the explanation, in the grand words of a wise man who lived nearly three centuries ago, to "Time, the Discoverer of the Truth."

CHAPTER IV.

PATENT STILLS AND SILENT SPIRITS.

WE have already explained that when a fermented mash is distilled in a pot-still, the product contains not only alcohol and water but also a number of flavouring matters, vegetable oils and essences, yielded by the substances from which the mash was made, and that these flavouring matters serve to differentiate spirit obtained from different sources, and to declare the character of the mash. Not to speak of minor distinctions, spirit distilled from a grape mash is brandy, and has distinctive characters of its own. Spirit distilled from a malt or grain mash is Whisky, and also has distinctive characters. Spirit distilled from a cane sugar mash is rum, and could scarcely be mistaken for anything else. When the raw materials of the distillation are themselves of good quality, we obtain from them good brandy, or good Whisky, or good rum, as the case may be; and these products require only time and maturity to bring them to perfection. If, on the other hand, the raw materials are partially spoilt, or ill-flavoured, or in any way inferior, we still obtain from them brandy, or Whisky, or rum, but the quality of the product is inferior, in a degree determined by the inferiority of the source from which it was obtained. If the product, although inferior, is drinkable and market-

able, it will command a certain price as a spirit of
second or third-rate quality ; but, if it is not drinkable,
it must be in some way altered before it can be sold.
For this purpose it is submitted to a process called
rectification, which essentially consists in re-distillation,
with the addition of certain chemical solvents, chiefly
of an alkaline nature, which serve to retain some or all
of the objectionable matters in the body of the still,
and to prevent them from passing over with the new, or
second, or rectified product.   Now, there are some
original conditions of the spirit in which the taint to be
removed is only slight, and in which it can be removed
without at the same time removing the peculiar cha-
racteristics of the brandy, or Whisky, or rum, as the
case may be ; or, in other words, there are varieties of
brandy and of Whisky and of rum which may be
improved by slight rectification without loss of their
distinctive characters. Something disagreeable has been
taken out of them, and they are still what they were
before,' not of first-class quality, but better for the
process to which they have been subjected, and still
marketable.   Again, there are certain varieties which
are so nasty, or so deeply tainted from the faults of the
raw material, that the taint can only be removed by a
degree and amount of rectification which removes the
distinctive characters also; and then we no longer have
rectified brandy, or rectified Whisky, or rectified rum,
but only rectified spirit, from which everything distinctive of brandy, or Whisky, or rum, has been taken
away in the process which it has undergone.   Rectified
spirit is a great solvent of vegetable matters, and also a
great preservative of them, and hence it is much used
in medicine to make the preparations known as tinc-
tures.   It is kept by all dispensing chemists, and may

be sold by them in small quantities without a spirit
licence. It should consist of nearly equal parts of
absolute alcohol and water; and the best way to
become acquainted with its qualities is to buy a little
from some chemist and to examine it. It is a limpid,
colourless, highly inflammable liquid, which quickly
dries up or evaporates, and which should leave no smell
behind. It has what is described as a penetrating odour,
but this is not really an odour, but a stimulation of
the lining membrane of the nostrils by the irritating
vapour. Alcohol has a great craving or affinity for water;
and the rectified spirit, although it has received some
water, has not received enough to satisfy this craving,
so that it seeks to withdraw more from the moist tissues
of the body whenever it comes in contact with them. It
is by thus attracting the water of the tissues that it
irritates, and that it seems pungent to the nose, and hot
to the tongue or throat, when tasted or swallowed.
The action of the substances called caustics is, generally
speaking, of a similar character; that is to say, they
produce smarting, or heat, and ultimately destroy the
living tissues, by abstracting their water from them.
Besides being the basis of many medicines of which it
forms a permanent part, rectified spirit is very useful as
a solvent in extracting the active parts of certain
medicinal plants, such as morphia and quinine, and its
power as a solvent of gums renders it of much value as
a basis of varnishes and other preparations. The high
price placed upon it by the excise duty was for many
years practically prohibitory of its employment in this
country for purposes for which it is essential; and hence
certain industries which were largely carried on in France
could not be carried on in England, on account of the
cost of the necessary spirit. This difficulty has been

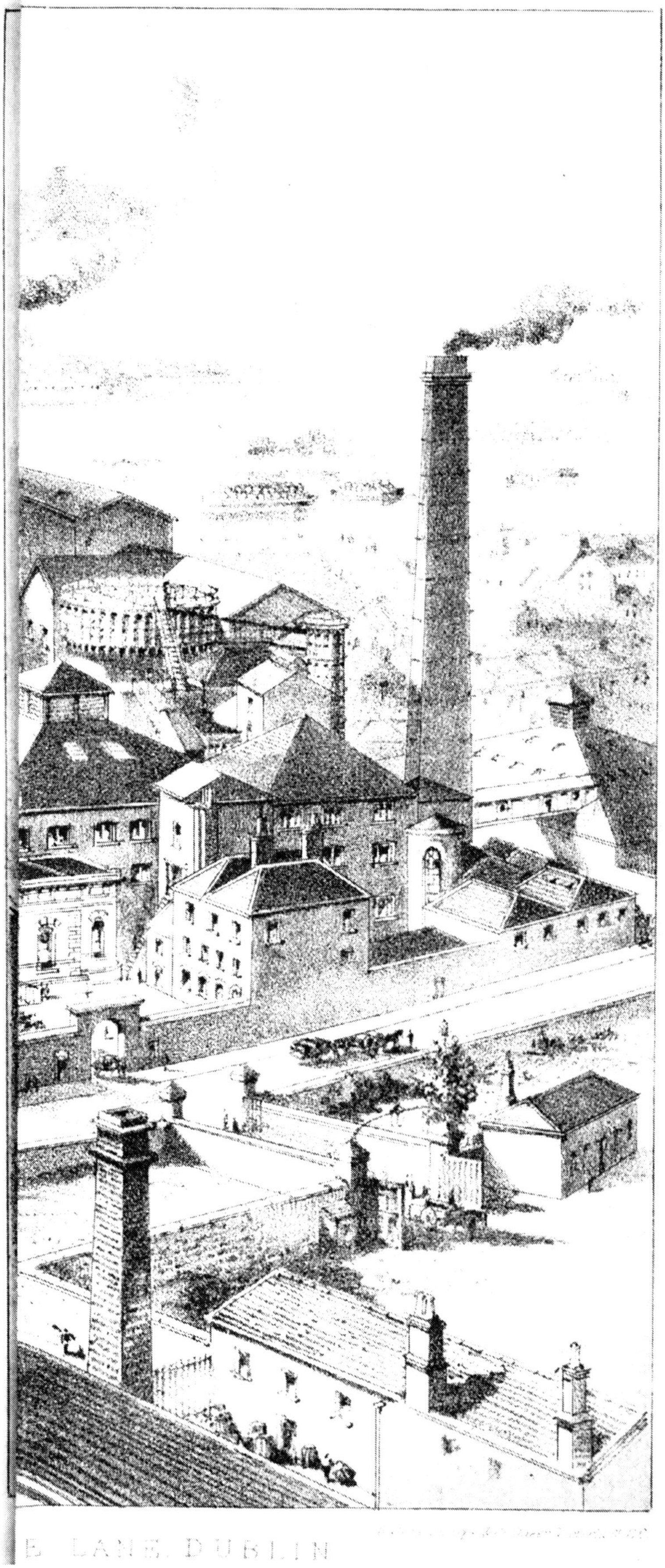

E LANE, DUBLIN

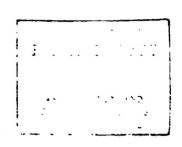

overcome of late years by the discovery that spirit may be impregnated with an offensive substance called "Methyl," which cannot be removed by rectification, and which is so nauseous that it cannot be drunk, but which does not in the least diminish the solvent qualities. This methylated spirit is allowed to be sold duty free, being wholly unfit for human consumption; and it has rendered possible the unrestrained employment of spirit in the arts, and has also, therefore, enormously increased the demand. Nearly fifty years ago, a Mr. Coffy invented a still which may be roughly described as intended to combine, in its action, the two processes of distillation and of rectification—by sending over alcohol and water alone, and by arresting or destroying all the flavouring matters which are derived from the mash, and are sent over in pot-still distillation. For many years this invention remained comparatively little utilised, because the demand for rectified spirit was limited; but, with the increasing demand for various purposes which was incidental to many improvements in industrial processes, it soon became apparent that many sources of starch and sugar, although wholly useless for making spirit which would retain the flavour of the mash, would be perfectly and cheaply available for making spirit intended to be flavourless; and so the patent still became the recipient of a great many matters which had previously been wasted; and it succeeded in making spirit from them all. In its earlier days there were a good many failures, or partial failures; that is to say, the still allowed matters to pass over which it should have retained. This was not a fault of the invention, but was a result of carelessness in using it; and it has been gradually, but not altogether, set aside by experience.

In spite of experience, workmen will sometimes be careless; and some unknown Scotch distillers, who wrote to
the *Times* in February, 1876, complained, simply and
piteously, that their patent still products were sometimes very nasty, and fit only for methylation. In other
words, their workmen were ignorant or careless, and
the spirit, instead of being "silent," told tales of its origin.
As a rule, however, due care and skill being assumed,
the patent still sends over what is practically a rectified
spirit, having no distinctive qualities, telling no tales to
nose or palate of the source from which it was obtained,
and hence, in the almost poetic language of the trade,
commonly called " Silent " spirit. The owner of a
patent still, therefore, instead of being confined, like a
Whisky distiller, to the use of the best materials, which
would command a high price for various purposes, is
able to make his spirit from anything that comes to
hand, and with little reference to any other quality
than cheapness. The manufacture of silent spirit is
practically based upon the utilisation of waste products.
We have already hinted at some of these waste products, and we are unable even to attempt to enumerate
all of them. From time to time, some enterprising
distiller finds out some new raw material, and keeps
his secret as long as he can. Occasionally, no doubt,
more especially in dealing with new material, the
patent still tells tales, and produces spirit fit only
for methylation; but difficulties hence arising are merely
stimulants to manufacturing ingenuity and enterprise.
In no long time after the general employment of the
patent still, a spirit perfectly silent, a simple rectified
spirit, could be produced at much less than the cost of
Whisky; and this was speedily used to adulterate the
Whisky of the Dublin houses on its way from the

maker to the consumer. Sometimes, no doubt, the products of patent still distillation were not quite without character; but it is manifest that they might bear traces of their origin and yet not be so vilely flavoured as to be necessarily used only for the preparation of methylated spirit. As a rule, the samples were such as would have passed muster with a chemist for rectified spirit; and they would have, properly speaking, no taste, but only the alcoholic penetration and pungency. Such spirit would no more be Whisky than it would be brandy or rum, although it would contain the alcohol which is a necessary ingredient in all these liquids, and would possess the solvent power necessary in order to take up and retain flavours when these were artificially added in the after processes of manufacture. If was a mere basis, a foundation, plastic to the hand to the compounder, and capable of being converted into sham Whisky, or sham brandy, or sham rum, as well as into honest doctors' stuff or into good varnish. As no one could ascertain by any examination of the product what was the material from which it was derived, so it contained nothing which could undergo any spontaneous maturation or development; and being silent spirit, approximately pure alcohol and water on the day when it was manufactured, it remained absolutely without change, save that it would lose strength by evaporation for any period of time. As we have seen already, all pot-still spirit steadily improves by keeping, and improves in quality far more than it deteriorates in strength; so that a Whisky originally twenty-five over proof, and worth, say, four shillings a gallon, if kept for ten years, or until it had fallen by evaporation of spirit barely to proof strength, would have gained very much more in value by its

D

higher quality than it would have lost by its reduction
in alcohol. It is therefore worth while to keep Whisky,
but in the case of silent spirit there is no beneficial change to balance or exceed the loss of strength
by age; and hence there is not only no inducement to
keep such spirit, but every possible inducement to be
rid of it as quickly as possible, on the very day of dis_
tillation, if circumstances will permit. It is then as
well-flavoured as it ever will be, and stronger than it
ever will be again. The dealers in sham Whisky,
therefore, when they advertise " age " as one of the
qualities of their precious compounds, are advancing
what they well know to be a statement wholly opposed
to the truth, since the prosperity of their business and
the lowness of their prices essentially rest upon selling
without delay, and upon the activity of what they term
"the nimble sixpence." Of course it is possible that
there may be, here and there, private customers, or
even publicans, who are so little aware of the nature of
sham Whisky that they lay it down to improve by
time; and, as hope is the mother of credulity, it is even
possible that some of these confiding persons may
imagine that their hoard has earned interest upon their
outlay. In this belief, however, they are totally and
lamentably deceived. As we shall have to show hereafter, it is quite possible that sham Whisky may
undergo some deterioration, at least in the sense of
being even less like the real spirit than it was when it
was first made; but it is impossible that under any
circumstances it can improve. The consumers, if such
there be, who like it and drink it knowingly, may
comfort themselves with the knowledge that it is as
good when fetched in a pitcher from the neigh-
bouring public-house, as it would be if bottled

by themselves, and kept religiously even for generations.

To recapitulate what has already been advanced, we may repeat that silent spirit is distilled from all sorts of materials, in a still which has the property of preventing the peculiar characters of these materials from coming over and asserting themselves; so that the product of a successful distillation is simply rectified spirit, pure alcohol and water, or nearly so, without distinctive flavour or quality, and without capacity for improvement. It is worth, on an average, about two shillings a gallon, and it can be obtained from some foreign countries at a still lower price. There has lately been a Russian silent spirit in the market, at a price of eleven-pence a gallon, the sources of which are not generally known. It is obvious that a spirit distilled from first-class grain or malt, by a process requiring the closest skilled supervision and a very costly plant, can never compete, as regards mere cost, with even the native products of patent still distillation.

CHAPTER V.

THE GROWTH OF SILENT SPIRIT INTO SHAM WHISKY.

IN nearly every anatomical museum there lingers a
grim story, dating from before the days of methylation,
of some former porter or other custodian or servant,
whose wont it was to obtain the means of inexpensive
inebriation by drinking the spirit out of the preparation
jars.   In those days, good rectified spirit was used for
preparations; and the value of the duty-paid spirit in a
large museum, and the cost of replacing the annual loss
by evaporation, even if not by drinking, was enormous.
At present, nothing but methylated spirit is used for
such purposes, and it is not only comparatively cheap,
but so nasty that as yet no porter has been suspected of
drinking it.   Even in the old days, the taste which thus
displayed itself was one to be marvelled at, for the
taste of rectified spirit is not inviting; and, if it were
offered to the public, even under the name of Whisky,
in its pure or natural state, it would probably find but
few purchasers.   Of this, anyone may convince himself
by buying a little rectified spirit at a chemist's shop, and
by tasting it both in a pure and in a diluted condition.
Accordingly, the attempt to sell silent spirit for Whisky
was not made all at once, but only by slow degrees.   In
the first instance, a dealer would buy from a provincial
distillery a thousand gallons or so of a coarse, new,

strongly tasted genuine Irish pot-still Whisky, and, at
some bonded warehouse, say at Belfast, would mix—we
beg pardon, would " *blend* "— this with another thousand gallons of silent spirit, imported for the purpose;
he would then have two thousand gallons of a liquid
which he would sell under the name of Whisky. The
real Whisky in the mixture would, perhaps, be worth
4s. 6d. per gallon, and the silent spirit would, perhaps,
be worth 2s. 6d. The former would be too strongly
tasted, the latter would have no taste at all. It is
obvious that the effect of mixing the two would be to
produce a milder liquid than the genuine Whisky
employed, and that the mixture might be passed off as
having greater age, or originally better quality, than it
really possessed. It must be observed that there would
be no real improvement, because the strong flavours of
the real Whisky would not have been decomposed or
otherwise modified by time, but only disguised by dilution; although it must be conceded that, if these flavours
were hurtful, as there would be less of them in a given
quantity of the mixture, this would be more wholesome
than the young Whisky which was used. Unless with
very skilled buyers, however, the general effect would
be to make the mixture appear to be Whisky of better
quality and greater value even than that of the moiety
of real Whisky which it would contain; and so, assuming
the moiety of Whisky to be worth £225, and the moiety
of silent spirit to be worth £125, the two together might
attain a selling value of, say, £500, as a mere result of
the mixture. The value would, of course, be a deceptive and not a real value; or, in other words, the
mixture would not be worth £500, but would only be
capable of being represented to be so to those
unacquainted with the way in which it had been pro-

duced. The betrayal of the secret would have destroyed
the augmentation of value. The chief evil of this
practice was that it threw into circulation, for drinking
purposes, a quantity of young Whisky which contained.
fusel-oil and other impurities which time would have
removed, which was not really fit for consumption, but
which was rendered acceptable to consumers by being
diluted with silent spirit. The fusel-oil and such like
matters have been accused, we do not say whether
rightly or wrongly, but, at all events, very often and
very decidedly, of being far more injurious to the
human organism than the alcohol which suspends or
dissolves them; and it is affirmed that young and imma-
ture Whisky occasions a peculiarly insubordinate and
violent form of drunkenness. The venerable story of
the old Scotchman, who palliated a row on a Sunday by
explaining that "The Whusky war that bad, that the
lads had nae respect for the Sawbath-day," although
venerable, is none the less the expression of a belief
that still endures, and much of the violence of the
intoxication of our large towns has constantly been
ascribed to the adulterated and bad quality of the spirit
sold at common public-houses. To quote a happy
phrase which was lately used by a correspondent of
the *Times*, this violent drunkenness is a result not of
alcohol, but of more noxious matters combined with it;
it is, strictly speaking, poisoning intoxication, and not
inebriation or mere drunkenness. To return from this
digression to the ways and works of the "blenders,"
we may say briefly that these persons were soon found
engaged in the development of their new business; and
they tried a vast number of curious and instructive
experiments in their endeavour to solve the great
problem of how bad and how inexpensive a liquid

might be substituted for Whisky, and yet palmed off upon the unsuspecting public. We have before us the records of many "blends," some of them containing silent spirit from a single source, some containing five or six varieties, perhaps added together for the convenience of dealing at once with several job lots, some containing none but provincial Whisky, others containing a small quantity of genuine Dublin Whisky, but none of them open to the charge of extravagance in the use made of the last-named costly ingredient. Fortunately, particulars of all the blends are officially recorded, and those who know how to proceed may obtain a full account of them. We subjoin the particulars in four instances, which will serve to illustrate the sort of thing which is done every day. Only one of them, however, is a mixture of the comparatively innocent kind to which we have as yet referred; and one, to which we shall come in its turn, contains no Whisky at all.

The mixture to which we will first call attention, and which may be described as No. 1, was made in Dublin in December, 1875. It contained:—

Spirit, presumably silent, from Haig, Cameron Bridge 1173.6 Galls.
    ,,   ,,   ,,   ,,   Watt, Derry ...   ... 479.2 ,,
    ,,   ,,   ,,   ,,   Walker, Limerick ... 753.2 ,,
Provincial Whisky, from Daly, Tullamore ... ... 1554.4 ,,
    ,,   ,,   ,, Devereux, Wexford ... 1958.2 ,,
Dublin Whisky, John Power and Son   ... ... 786.0 ,,

                                     6704.6 ,,

It will be observed that, in this instance, we have 3512.6 gallons of provincial Whisky, presumably of no great age, since otherwise it would not have borne dilution, and that this was diluted with more than two-thirds of its bulk (2406 gallons) of silent spirit.

In this way the strong taste of the Whisky would be brought down without diminishing its alcoholic strength, and a fictitious appearance of greater age and better quality than it possessed would be conferred upon it. It was probably intended that the result should pass muster as Whisky with purchasers who had some faint notion of the meaning of the word, and of the characters which the genuine article ought to possess; and so, in order to improve the imitation, or to render the resemblance more deceptive, a modicum of real Dublin Whisky, from John Power and Son, and in the proportion of no less than 786 gallons to 5918.6 gallons, or a little more than 13 per cent., was added as a finishing touch to the compound. We shall find hereafter that there would be nothing remarkable or unusual in the occurrence if this " blend " had been put into old casks of John Power and Son, and had been sold as their Whisky; although in the particular instance we have no reason for suspecting that such was the case. However it was sold, such was its composition; and it is this sort of combination of a great deal of silent spirit with a small quantity of Whisky which dealers describe to their customers and the public as the last result of years of study, and of the highest refinement of skill, and which they represent as being better—Heaven save the mark!—than the genuine Whisky to which it owes the only merit it can possess. It is perfectly plain that the only motive for bringing 1173 gallons of silent spirit from Scotland to Dublin, and the only motive for bringing 1232 gallons from Derry and Limerick to Dublin was that all this might be made to appear to be of Dublin manufacture. It would all be shipped to England under a Dublin permit; and to obtain this permit, in support, or apparent support, of a false pretence, the makers were ready to pay freight and carriage for the whole of the 5918 gallons which they had collected together to receive a character from the 786 gallons of real Dublin Whisky which they were so extravagant as to throw into their witches' cauldron. We confidently appeal to the common sense of the public for an answer to the question whether this class of dealing falls far short of fraud.

Blend No. 2, to which we shall next direct attention, differs from the foregoing in containing no Irish spirit at all, except a minute proportion, probably a chance residue, amounting to 298. gallons in a total of over 8000. It was thus composed :—

Spirit, presumably silent, from Menzies and Co., Edinburgh ... ... 2989.7 Galls.

,,	,,	,,	,,	Haig, Cameron Bridge	1623.6	,,
,,	,,	,,	,,	Harvey, Glasgow ...	2120.7	,,
,,	,,	,,	,,	MacFarlane, Glasgow	1162.5	,,
,,	,,	,,	,,	Watt, Derry	298.8	,,

8195.3

This second blend was made in the same month as the preceding one, and by the same firm of dealers but, before we enter upon the question of the precise significance of its composition, we must say something about the extent and manner in which similar practices are carried on at Belfast. where upwards of 3,000,000 gallons of British spirits were blended in the year 1875, before being sent out for consumption. We subjoin two examples, for which we are able to give the dates at which the several parcels of spirit were warehoused, and thus to show to what extent the question of age enters into these mixtures.

Blend No. 3 was composed almost entirely of presumably silent spirit. It was made in Belfast, on the 29th of September, 1875; and it will be observed that the whole of the spirit employed was imported, that all of it had been imported within six weeks, and all but one small parcel within three weeks :—

BLEND No. 3.

Gallons	From	Warehoused
534.7	Walker and Co., Limerick	... Aug. 16, 1875.
373.0	Menzies and Co., Edinburgh	... Sept. 8, ,,
149.4	Stewart and Co., Kirkliston	... ,, 18, ,,
1122.7	Harvey and Co., Glasgow	... ,, 18, ,,
406.3	Stewart and Co., Paisley ...	... ,, 24, ,,
672.6	Stewart and Co., Kirkliston	... ,, 24, ,,
1505.4	Preston and Co., Liverpool	... ,, 24, ,,
341.5	Stewart and Co., Kirkliston	... ,, 28, ,,

Total 5105.6

Blend No. 4 contains spirit of quite respectable antiquity. For some unintelligible reason, but perhaps on account of slackness of the market, some of it had been in stock five months, and all of it at least four months. Here it is—the time and place of mixture being Belfast, June the 9th, 1875 :—

BLEND No. 4.

Gallons	From	Warehoused
644.1	Bruce, Comber	... Jan. 19, 1875.
129.2	,, ,, ...	... Feb. 1, ,,
129.5	,, ,, ...	... ,, 1, ,,
1925.2	MacFarlane and Co., Glasgow	... ,, 4, ,,
1296.3	Walker and Co., Liverpool...	... ,, 4, ,,
1023.5	,, ,, ...	... ,, 4, ,,
1269.4	Menzies and Co., Edinburgh	... ,, 3, ,,

Total 6417.2

In these three last blends it will be seen we have a total of 19,718.1 gallons, in which only three parcels, of 298.8, of 534.7, and of 902.8 gallons respectively, were Irish at all, and that two of these three parcels were not made at the place of blending, at Dublin or at Belfast, but were sent there in order to receive the advantage, if such it is to be considered, of a Dublin or a Belfast permit. The rest of the 20,000 gallons, using round numbers, was all Scotch or English spirit; and upon all this the dealers had gone to the trouble and expense of taking it to Ireland only to bring it back again. The course of action which we have traced out with regard to this 20,000 gallons we could trace out equally well, did time and space permit, with regard to millions of gallons more, but to do so would be tedious, and would lead to no useful purpose. The four blends given above are those of which we have previously published the particulars in a pamphlet which has been widely circulated, and with such information that every one in the trade may easily see by what firms they were put together; but the accuracy of our account of them has remained absolutely unchallenged, except that, in the former edition of this work, we fell into the error of considering that the 902.8 gallons supplied by Messrs. Bruce, of Comber, near Belfast, and incorporated in blend No. 4, were to be reckoned as Scotch spirit. It will be manifest that this very trivial inaccuracy leaves the case substantially unchanged, and in no way affects the general argument, and it is mainly for this reason that we adduce the same examples again. The object of the whole proceeding was to sell Scotch or English silent spirit under the name of Irish, and, if we mistake not, under the name of *old* Irish Whisky; and we shall presently see that the fraud which taints the very inception of such a scheme has to assume a still more aggravated form before its aims can be perfectly achieved. Even with a Dublin or Belfast permit, silent spirit in its natural state cannot be sold for Whisky; and, therefore, when there is no Whisky in the compound, an attempt must be made to imitate the taste and appearance of Whisky by other means.

The only preparation to which genuine Whisky is subjected, if preparation it may be called, is that it is generally suffered to mature in sherry casks. For this purpose, these casks are bought up from wine importers, and the Whisky derives from them a certain colour, and perhaps also a certain vinous flavour, which it would not otherwise possess. The fact that sherry casks are so used has become a piece of popular knowledge; and hence consumers expect Dublin Whisky, or, as they now generally call it, Irish Whisky, to have some indication of a sherry flavour; and here, in passing, we should call attention to this question of name—Irish or Dublin—which is one of more importance to the present question than it might at first sight appear. When the Whisky made by our firms gained its great reputation, it was, of course, "Dublin" Whisky; but, as it was almost the only Irish Whisky exported, or known out of the country in which it was produced, it was in those days quite sufficiently described as "Irish" Whisky, the word Irish being used especially to distinguish it from the Scotch sort, which, as we have already shown on the authority of Dr. Johnson, was less highly esteemed. Now, however, since smaller distillers of Whisky have sprung up in the Irish provincial towns, making what is undeniably Irish Whisky; and more especially since patent stills have been erected in Belfast and elsewhere, making what is undeniably Irish silent spirit, and is sold under the name of Irish Whisky, we are anxious to impress upon consumers that the equivalent for the " Irish " Whisky of the last generation is the " Dublin " Whisky of to-day; and that they must ask for Dublin Whisky if they wish to secure the legitimate successor of the spirit which originally made the name of " Whisky " so famous.

Returning from this digression to the sherry question, and to the supposed vinous flavour of Irish Whisky, it would, of course, be quite open to the makers of silent spirit to put their product also into sherry casks; and, so far, to confer upon it the desired appearance and flavour. To do this, however, would require that the silent spirit should remain in the sherry casks for a considerable time, during which time it would be losing alcoholic strength, and would be doing nothing to promote the evolutions of that "nimble sixpence" to which we have referred. The ingenuity of blenders when met by this difficulty was not long in discovering what seemed to them a more excellent way. There are certain places in the Mediterranean, Cette, and others, where an enormous business is carried on in manufacturing artificial wines; and in manufacturing, among other like compounds, an imitation of the worst public-house sherry. The liquid thus produced is commonly known in this country as " Hamburgh " sherry, from its principal port of shipment for our shores; and those who watch the course of such transactions were at one time much puzzled to explain how it happened that so much Hamburgh sherry went to Ireland. The *Times* removed this difficulty by explaining that it was used as one of the ingredients for converting silent spirit into sham

Whisky; and a denial of this statement, made by an anonymous correspondent, led to a controversy which brought the general state of the facts clearly to light. It must be premised that the Hamburgh sherry, the precise composition of which can be known only to those who make it, is supposed not to contain any wine at all, but to be wholly artificial or fictitious; and also that it cannot be added to the silent spirit while this is in bond, but only after duty has been paid and the spirit delivered to the owner. Hamburgh sherry, whatever it may be made of, is recognised as wine by the Custom authorities, and is admitted as wine, at a duty of half-a-crown a gallon, so long as it does not contain more than 42 per cent. of proof spirit; while the duty on spirit is 10s. the proof gallon, or 12s. 6d. per gallon for spirit 25 per cent. over proof. 100 gallons of such spirit at the 12s. 6d. duty, mixed with 100 gallons of Hamburgh sherry at 58 under proof, and at 2s. 6d. per gallon duty, would yield 200 gallons of a mixture 16 or 17 under proof—the strength at which bottled Whisky is usually sold—and at a duty of only 7s. 6d. per gallon, or a saving of tenpence farthing per gallon in duty alone. Putting the matter in another way, we find that the fraudulent Whisky dealer may make a profit of £7 2s. 6d. per butt on all the Hamburgh sherry that he can mix. The butt of 108 gallons of Hamburgh sherry, containing 45 gallons of proof spirit, would cost £9 to purchase, and £13 10s. for duty; so that the purchaser would receive 45 gallons of duty-paid proof spirit for £22 10s. or at a total cost of 10s. per gallon, and would have 63 gallons of water, containing sugar, colour, and flavouring thrown into the bargain. Now 45 gallons of silent proof spirit in any other form would cost 10s. 2d. per gallon duty, and 3s. per gallon to purchase; in all £29 12s. 6d., or £7 2s. 6d. more than the same quantity of spirit when bought as Hamburgh sherry. The 63 gallons of water would not be surplusage, partly because they are required for the dilution of the silent spirit, and partly because they contain the particular flavour which renders the artificial sherry valuable in the manufacture, even apart from the pecuniary saving effected by its employment.

We have not the least idea what Hamburgh sherry is made of; and, although we can well imagine that a connoisseur in wine would say of it, as the late Lord Derby did of some cheap claret which was sent to him. that he would rather have gout than drink it, yet we are not aware that it has ever been proved to be particularly deleterious. It must not be supposed, however, that artificial Whisky-making consists only of the simple process of adding Hamburgh sherry to silent spirit. This is only a first stage, and one which requires to be supplemented by processes of a much more elaborate character. There has arisen of late years a body of persons whose business is conducted without parade, but who call themselves brewers' chemists, or distillers' chemists, or vintners' chemists, as the case may be. These men make and sell a variety of mixtures, the composition of which is known only to themselves, for giving any desired flavour or appearance to any alcoholic drink; and we think it may fairly be inferred that their ingenuity is always a little in advance of the suspicions or the knowledge of the public. However this may be, it is at least certain that the tradesmen to whom we have referred keep two classes of compounds—some which they sell openly, and even advertise largely, and some which are kept in back cupboards, and are reserved for customers with whom they have established confidential relations. A liquid called "prune wine" and a liquid called "sherry essence," and a first cousin of Hamburgh sherry named "Malaga," can be bought across the counter by anyone who chooses to inquire for them; but behind these there are, no doubt, a variety of ingredients which would startle any consumer of so-called Whisky who chanced to light upon them, and which, if harmless, are only rendered so by the extent to which they are diluted by the time they reach the tumbler. It is probable that creosote, or its kindred preparations, are sometimes used; but perhaps in making sham Scotch Whisky rather than sham Irish, since Irish Whisky is free from the smoky taste which is one of the supposed qualities of the Scotch variety. There has lately been a large increase in the importation of methylated spirit, called purified naphtha, or spirit of methyl; and the Customs authorities, who are not quite sure what becomes of this increase, are not without uneasy suspicions that it may find its way into the so-called Whisky trade. When purified to any extent short of potability it is admitted free of duty; and it is quite possible that, when not potable of itself, it may yet be potable when sufficiently diluted, and that it may thus come into use as a flavouring ingredient. It must be remembered that, in the present day, the art of adulteration is placed upon a thoroughly scientific basis; that it is not conducted by petty thieves who lurk in obscure hiding-places, but by persons of considerable wealth and of apparent respectability, who often permanently retain clever chemists to assist them in their nefarious practices, and to keep them ahead of the progress constantly made in the art of detecting their devices; and the resources of fraud are being constantly increased by the ingenuity of those who make a business and a profit of applying them.

It may well be asked, under these circumstances, how is it possible for the consumer to protect himself, or to distinguish genuine Dublin Whisky from fraudulent imitations? To do so is not difficult, when once a knowledge of the standard has been gained, because the utmost cleverness of adulterators has never yet succeeded in making anything which would pass muster as Whisky among those who know the characters and qualities of the genuine product. Genuine Whisky, of mature age, is a really exquisite perfume, a bottle of which, when first opened, fills the room with its fragrance. A few drops of it poured upon a pocket-handkerchief, or rubbed over the palms of the hands, remain fragrant until the whole has evaporated and the last trace of odour has disappeared; while sham Whisky, similarly treated, leaves behind what can only be adequately described as a stink. A similar test may be applied by mixing the liquids with equal parts of cold water, and smelling them after a few minutes have been suffered to elapse. The genuine Whisky, thus treated, offers the same perfume as before; and also, both to nose and palate, a character of oneness which is more easily appreciated than described. There is no breaking up of the general odour into component parts, and no change in its quality, except that it becomes gradually fainter as it dies away. With sham Whisky, on the contrary, we obtain, by dilution, a struggle between five or six nasty smells, which have been divorced from all union by dilution, and which are produced by ingredients of different degrees of volatility, so that one of them, and that generally the odour of rectified spirit, survives the complete disappearance of all the rest. We

E

are about to make arrangements which will render it more easy than heretofore for the public to obtain our several varieties of Whisky; and, although we cannot supply any quantity of spirit at an age which has brought it to complete maturity, and developed all its high qualities to the utmost, such spirit being obviously a luxury which, like very old wine, consumers must secure for themselves by the exercise of due foresight, yet our ordinary brands will show the differences, when compared with sham Whisky, which are pointed out above; and there can be no more amusing experiment for anyone who takes interest in the question, than to obtain some dozen or so of samples of Whisky from dealers and taverns in his neighbourhood, and to submit them to the dilution test in a row, comparing one with another. After a very few such experiments there is no one with senses of ordinary acuteness who would have any difficulty in distinguishing genuine from sham Whisky when blindfolded, and without the smallest other clue to the nature of each. We shall have to mention, in the sequel, the means which we have adopted in order to afford the public easy and certain access to a standard of quality by which their judgment may be safely guided.

It cannot be a matter of surprise that the sale of fictitious Whisky has been made the basis of fictitious reputations; and, as we have already indicated, some of the best known names in the trade are those of dealers who never made any Whisky in their lives, but who have advertised that they had for sale Whisky which they described as theirs, and which was theirs only in the sense that they had bought it and paid for it. Allowing for the ordinary profits of the trade, genuine Dublin Whisky cannot be sold retail at less than 42s. per dozen bottles; and there are many samples

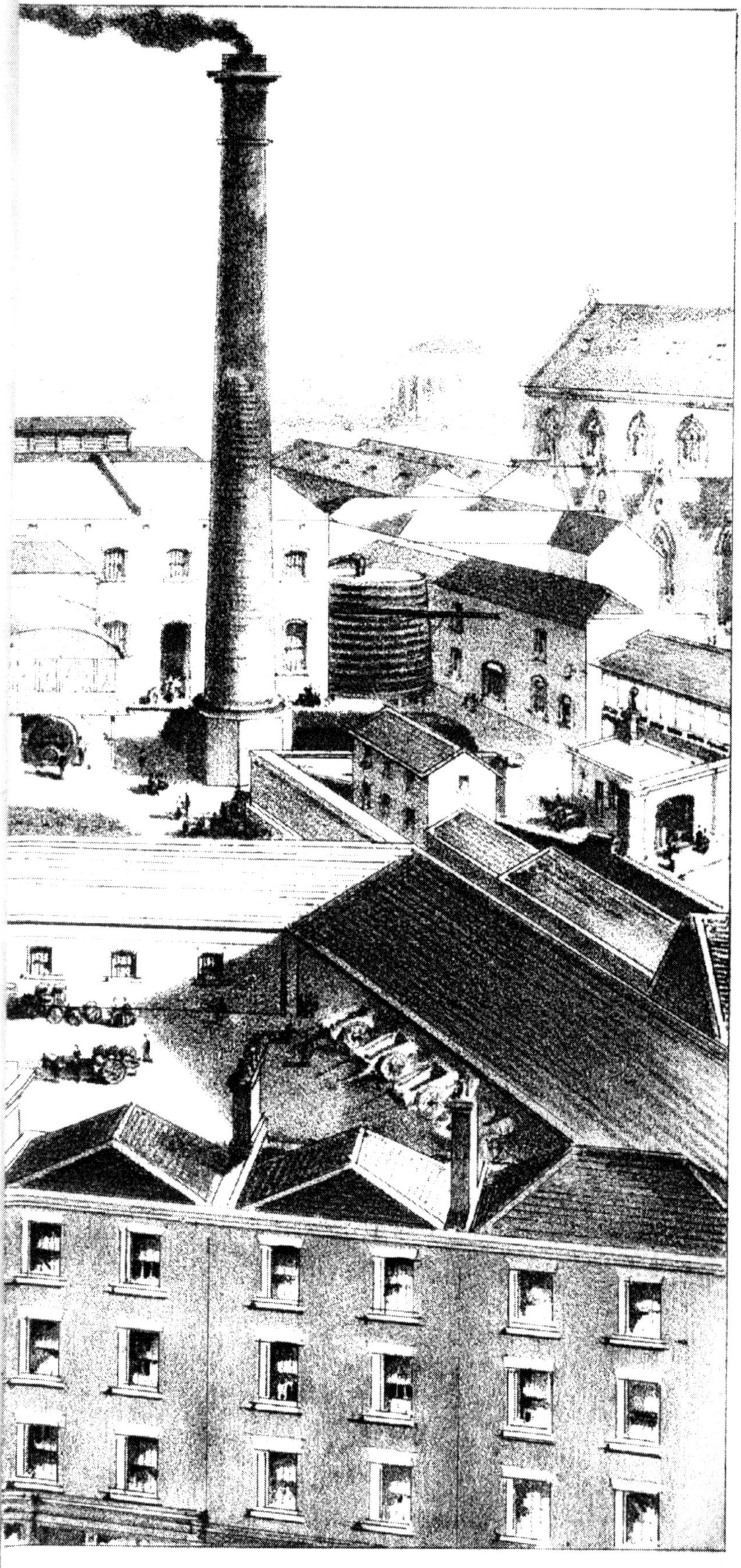

'S LANE, DUBLIN

which would fetch a still higher price. If the public would once realise the simple facts that the best Whisky can only be made from the best grain, and that it requires, when made, to be matured by time, they would in due sequence argue that the best grain costs money, that the lying idle of this money for two or three years involves loss of interest, and that all this has to be paid for; so that if the due price is not charged there must be some deception in the commodity. We have defined Whisky; and purchasers have only to consider whether Whisky can be produced, even without reference to the cost of extensive advertising, at the price at which so many of the imitations of it are sold. These imitations, doubtless, have their uses; and must continue to be made, probably, in large and increasing quantities. It has been well said that shoddy has its merits, in that it places a woollen garment within the reach of many persons who otherwise could not afford one; and the same will apply to silent spirit, which should hold, in the cellars of the publican, the place which was assigned to "South African" wine in the famous ballad in which Hood described the landlady of a country inn, and the many attractions of her well-kept house, winding up with—

> " Besides all these, she kept in store,
> Cape for the meaner sort,
> Who did not mind the stomach-ache,
> And could not pay for port!"

This was all right enough; but if the landlady had given her Cape to her best customers she would have ruined her business, unless she could have persuaded them that it really was port, in which case she would have ruined the reputation of the wine. The latter course is that on which the spirit dealers seem bent. If they sold their stuff under its right name, or under any new names invented by themselves, nobody would have a right to complain of them, the spirit would stand or fall upon its merits, and would always, on account of its cheapness, be acceptable to the "meaner sort," whose palates are not rightly educated. But in selling this stuff under the name of Whisky they are guilty of a deliberate false pretence; for it is not Whisky, and is not even very much like it. They drag down the reputation of real Whisky to the level of the fictitious imitation; and they, probably, do not cause the inevitable consumption of their own brew among the poor to be increased by a single gallon. We are fully convinced that the false pretence gains nothing, and that it is hurtful alike to manufacturers and to the public.

CHAPTER VI.

THE RELATIVE WHOLESOMENESS OF WHISKY AND OF SILENT SPIRIT.

IN dealing with the question of the relative wholesomeness of different forms of spirit, it seems at first sight difficult to obtain any trustworthy data upon the point; because the members of the medical profession, to whom we are compelled to look for guidance upon such a question, are not agreed among themselves upon the larger question whether alcohol, in any of its forms, is wholesome at all; and a very small minority among their ranks goes so far as to say that it is, always and in all its forms, actively injurious. If we take the verdict of the great majority, it would be that alcohol in moderation is always harmless, and often necessary; but that, when taken in excess, it is a constant source of disease, and that it is more likely to be injurious the less it is diluted for habitual consumption. It is probable that a French or Spanish or Italian working man takes as much alcohol in a day as a London cab-driver; but the foreigners drink their alcohol in the form of wine, which is about one-fifth the strength of proof spirit, while the cabman drinks gin, which is about five-sixths the strength of proof spirit. The latter suffers from a variety of diseases induced by drink, especially from diseases of the liver and kidneys, from which the wine drinkers are comparatively free. The gin of the London cabman is silent spirit of the lowest order—of course flavoured to suit what is supposed to be his taste; and the records of any London hospital would show how it serves him. The wine-drinker, however, is not only taking his alcohol in a more diluted form, but he also takes it as it is furnished to him by the natural process of fermentation, and combined with certain vegetable matters which are well known to modify and assist its action upon the body. The alcohol of wine is always combined with various astringent substances, and with acids which form œnanthic ether by combining with part of the alcohol; and these things modify the general result in a way which Dr. Druitt in his Book on Wines has very happily described. He tells us how we get, in a glass of wine, practically the same ingredients, combined by nature, which a physician would be likely to prescribe if he wished to give a tonic and stimulating draught; and his parallel is so instructive that we subjoin it in his own words:—

"What is a light tonic? A little dilute acid, a slight bitter, a small quantity of some aromatic, a little alcohol, and some fragrant ether. This is just the mixture or draught that Nature has brewed ready to our hands."

Of the great power of the vinous ethers, we once heard a remarkable illustration. The landlord of a famous Paris restuarant, in looking over his cellar, found a few bottles of a wine originally of the highest quality and of great age, and he determined to signalise the discovery by drinking the contents of one of these bottles himself. It is well known that the quantity of œnanthic ether, or kindred compounds, contained in old wines varies as its quality, the value of the best varieties

being dependent, indeed, upon their capacity for form-
ing bouquet and flavour, which are only ether under
other names. The landlord retired to his private room
with his wine, and the servant who opened it remarked
its exquisite fragrance. An hour or two afterwards, the
toper not having come forth, his absence excited
remark, and he was found in a state of complete insensibility, produced by the ether which he had taken.
Ether, like alcohol, is a stimulant when taken in small
quantity, and when taken in larger quantities it produces an insensibility like that produced by chloroform,
and which is now constantly utilised, as being less
dangerous than the chloroform sleep for surgical purposes. But the ether intoxication, if so it may be
termed, differs from that produced by alcohol in being
unattended by any subsequent unpleasant or hurtful
consequences; and the mere stimulation produced by
ether would seem to be absolutely harmless. There is
therefore all the difference in the world between drinking mere raw spirit—silent spirit that is—robbed of all
the combinations in which it is presented to us by fermentation, and drinking a spirit which retains all these
combinations in their most essential and purest forms.
Beer and Burgundy, Whisky and Champagne, all alike
owe something of their properties to the alcohol which
they contain; but the differences between their several
modes of action upon the system are even greater than
the resemblances, and are fully sufficient to establish
the great importance, whether in medicine or in diet, of
the auxiliary substances with which alcohol is so closely
united and bound up. In Whisky, we have the alcohol
produced from certain cereals, together with the other
elements which these cereals afford; whereas, in silent
spirit, we have the bare alcohol, divorced from all its

proper and natural alliances, and stripped of the adju-
vants which so much promote its action. There is said
once to have been a nigger who professed entire indifference to the nature of his drink, so long only as it
would "make drunk come;" but there is no other point
of view from which it is possible to attain the same lofty
and sublime indifference. As we have already stated, a
great many of the so-called scientific experiments by
which it has been sought to determine the action of
alcoholic drinks, have been entirely vitiated by the
want of knowledge of the experimenters with regard to
the differences between these drinks when contrasted
with one another; and it would be impossible to draw
any inference with regard to the effects of Whisky,
with its ethers developed to the full extent by time,
from experiments made with silent spirit, which, even
though it might be in a bottle, with Whisky on the
label, would contain no ethers, and would possess no
capacity for developing them. On this point, however,
the experience of all physicians who have used alcoholic
stimulants intelligently, and without prejudice, is
uniform—namely, that their stimulating effects differ
directly as their quality and their maturity. In the
states of extreme weakness induced by fever, in which
life often hangs upon wine or brandy for days together,
no one in his senses, who had access to the finest
Cognac, or the most excellent port, would think of
administering British brandy or public-house particular.
It is unquestionable that the older wine or spirit,
although always and necessarily, from the mere fact of
its age, the weaker as far as mere alcohol is concerned,
is nevertheless the more stimulating and the more sus-
taining of the two, and this not, of course, from its
alcohol, but from the way in which that alcohol is sup-

ported by the other elements with which it is combined. We may appeal also to a still more widely spread experience, that is to say, to the effects of good and of bad wine or spirit upon the head, the tongue, and the digestion, on the morning after they have been consumed. There are few people, not having been "Good Templars" from their birth, who cannot relate how the glass of toddy or of wine which is pleasant and harmless at one house is hurtful and depressing at another; and, unless we were fully initiated into the arts of the wine makers of Cette and of the Whisky makers of Belfast, we could not pretend to say whether these effects were due to negative or to positive causes—due, that is, to the taking away of ingredients with which alcohol ought to be combined, or to the addition of flavouring matter by which it was hoped that the absence of these ingredients might be concealed. Sham wine-making and sham Whisky-making are still, in the words of the guilds of the Middle Ages, not only arts but mysteries; and they are mysteries of a kind into which we have no desire to penetrate.

Although the patent still spirit is ordinarily, and when the process of distillation has been well-managed, free from fusel oil and all analogous compounds, yet the necessary conditions of this freedom are not always observed, and then fusel oil may be present in large quantities, and a very noxious liquid may be the result, more especially when the mash has been largely composed of potatoes, whether rotten or otherwise. A curious evidence of this was afforded, at the Magherafelt Quarter Sessions, in January, 1870, when the Bo' Ness Distillery Company (Scotland), sued one John Magee, a publican, of Gulladuff, in the county of Londonderry, for the price of a cask of Whisky supplied to him, and for which he refused to pay, on account of the badness of its quality. The order of the cask from the Company's Belfast agent, and its delivery in the usual way, having been proved, the defendant said that he opened the cask the day he got it, and gave about a glass and a half of the spirit to a boy named Bradley. After drinking it Bradley leaped clean up off the ground, then threw himself down on his mouth and nose, and endeavoured to knock his brains out. When lying on the ground he wanted to eat the flesh off his arms. Four men had to go on their knees and hold him on the ground to prevent him from killing himself. A man named Magurk prepared an emetic; but, before it was given, Bradley vomited. He then recovered, and had no remembrance of anything that had occurred. The defendant sold some of the same Whisky to other parties that night, and they came back again and rebuked him for selling them such bad Whisky. He sold no more of it, but wrote the agent to come and take it back, which he did not do. He took a sample of the Whisky to Belfast, to be analysed by Dr. Hodges, who reported as follows :—

"I certify that a sample of Whisky, placed in my hands on the 25th of October, 1876, by Mr. John Magee, Gulladuff, for analysis, is contaminated by the presence of a large amount of fusel oil.

(Signed) "JOHN F. HODGES, M.D., F.C.S."

A second, and more extended report, was the following :—

"SIR,—I have examined the sample of Whisky, and find that the large amount of fusel oil which it contains explains the effects produced by it. This oil is found in new Whisky, but usually in very small quantities. A large amount may depend upon the distillation having been improperly conducted, or upon potatoes or other substances introduced into the mash. Fusel oil was the only injurious substance discovered.

(Signed) " JOHN HODGES."

It was further proved that the Whisky was only eleven over proof, although spirit twenty-four proof had been charged for; and that which produced the effects described had been reduced by the addition of one part of water to three. A witness who had purchased some of it deposed that he had taken it home and had given about half a glass to his son-in-law, who had been ill for a day or two afterwards. Other evidence was taken, and then the presiding magistrate gave judgment. He said, " He was clearly of opinion that the Whisky was unmarketable and unconsumable, and prejudicial to health. He was not learned enough in distillation to know accurately what proportions of the different substances from which Whisky was composed should be put in the distilling of it, but they all knew that if there was a large quantity of fusel oil in Whisky the results were most fearfully prejudicial to health. If the fusel oil was found in a large quantity in it, it was enough— he would not say to sicken—but to madden—positively to madden people to death. The result of coming to the conclusion which he had come to was that he must dismiss the process, because there was no sale sanctioned by law where the article was of such a description as to be incapable of being consumed without being absolutely injurious to the health of those who consumed it. A retailer had a right to get Whisky which would not ruin his trade, and would not poison the people. It was quite true, as everybody knew, that new Whisky must contain some fusel oil. Time dispersed it, and it evaporated and got away in such a manner as to prevent it being prejudicial to health; but that depended on the quantity; and Dr. Hodges, a man of very great experience and of very great eminence in Ireland, employed by Government for the purpose of making analyses and experiments whenever occasion required, certified that it was true that new spirit would contain small quantities of fusel oil in distillation, especially if the distillation was not properly conducted, or if substances such as potatoes were introduced into the mash. He certified also that potatoes would give it a large quantity of fusel oil, such as would produce the effects produced on Bradley. Now, he should say this, that the distillery company in that case should get possession at once of the cask of Whisky. Magee was bound to give it up, and they ought to get it and get it analysed, for their own mercantile credit and security, and see how the cask happened to be contaminated in the way in which it was described."

To take another example: a case was heard at the Marylebone Police Court, in April, 1876, in which a publican was summoned by the vestry of Paddington for selling adulterated Whisky. The parish analyst, Professor Anderson, to whom the sample was taken for analysis, said that "it contained foreign spirit otherwise than Whisky, and among its ingredients there was, in his opinion, methyl alcohol or wood spirit. It was a hot, not to say fiery, compound, and would certainly be injurious to the health of those who drank it. Some of the Whisky sold contained only a trace of Whisky, and if drank in large quantities was calculated to produce insanity."

We cannot leave this question of wholesomeness, however, without a glance also at the question of so-called purity. The patent-still people strip spirit of all that it ought to possess in addition to its bare alcohol, and then they claim merit for it on the ground of " purity." It would be more correct to say of the silent spirit that it is naked and not ashamed, than that it is " pure." As a man stripped of his garments is still a man, although not fit in such a state to enter into society, so the bare silent spirit is still spirit, but it is not fit for any of the dietetic uses to which spirit may be beneficially applied. The word " purity " is a very convenient one, especially when it is used to mislead people who have never thought about its meaning. Dr. Johnson defines " pure " to mean " unmingled, not altered by mixtures," a somewhat startling definition for professed " blenders," whose only claim to exist rests upon their power to alter their spirit by mixtures. The dealers, however, have lately taken the word " pure " into use to express freedom from fusel oil; perhaps not reflecting that, if fusel oil is a natural product of grain distillation, spirit, which neither contains it nor any of its secondary forms, cannot be called " pure," having been altered by deprivation of one or more of its natural constituents. The fact is that the word " pure," when applied to a compound substance of uncertain composition, is pure nonsense except in the single meaning that the substance in question has not been adulterated by the addition of foreign matters. We are quite willing to concede that much of the silent spirit of commerce is at least approximately

pure alcohol and water; and we go on to say that pure
alcohol and water is neither Whisky, nor fit for human
consumption. The truth with regard to what people
call fusel oil is, that this is a generic name for a great
number of compounds which are found in new Whisky,
and which form the basis of all the beneficial changes
which it undergoes in course of time, and of the flavours
and other high qualities which it develops. True
Whisky—pure Whisky, that is—contains either fusel oil
or some analogous compound when it is new; and, in
consequence of this, it is not acceptable until these
compounds have been broken up and re-arranged
by the spontaneous chemical action which occurs between them and the spirit with which they are
in contact. But it is the presence of these compounds, and the consequent possibility of the chemical
action between them and the surrounding alcohol, which
makes Whisky what it is; and a spirit which does not
contain them when it is new is not good for anything either then or at any future time. What is meant
by "pure"? If it is pure alchohol and water, it is not
Whisky at all; and, if it is not pure alcohol and water,
what additional flavouring or other substances does it
contain? and from whence have these been derived?
From barley? or malt? or oats? or from some wholly
extraneous source? It would be pleasant to obtain a
careful analysis of this liquid and of genuine Whisky,
showing their points of resemblance and of difference; but
that is something which we are not likely to obtain unless we undertake it ourselves. Even if we were to
undertake it, the results might be very indefinite; for
the flavours which combine with spirit are present in
very small quantities, besides being so fleeting, subtle,
and volatile, that they almost defy fixation and analysis,

and that they would only make a scarcely appreciable difference in the relative proportions of the ultimate constituents of the liquid. Practically speaking, the case is not one for genuine chemists; although it is well suited for puffs written by analysts who let themselves out for hire to manufacturers, and whose business it is to find nothing but all sorts of negative and positive excellences in the preparations made by their employers. It is a pity that the heads of the profession of chemistry, one which is every day becoming of more and more importance in the arts, cannot stop a use of chemical certificates which is degrading not only to those who issue them, but also to the general body to which such persons belong. There are some well-known analysts whose names are never advertised as testifying to the purity of somebody's black-lead or ginger-beer; but even the public utterances of these men are held of less account than they should be by reason of the facility with which chemical certificates about anything may be obtained, for advertising purposes, from men whose names are followed by all the letters of the alphabet. In order to know whether Whisky is pure or not, we should first require to have a complete analysis of a standard sample, or rather of standard samples taken at different ages; and the only pure Whisky would be such as, at corresponding ages, contained the same ingredients in something like the same proportions. Differences will be produced, of course, by varieties in the relative proportions of the several kinds of grain, barley, oats, and malted barley, from which any given sample has been distilled; and also, and even to a large extent, by slight variations in the fermenting process, or in the extent to which distillation has been pushed. Within the limits of strict purity, in so far as the word "purity" can be applied to Whisky, there is abundant room for considerable differences of character and even of quality; and such differences are inseparable from any process by which really pure Whisky can be manufactured. Uniformity of character and quality is only to be attained by taking the bare silent spirit, which is always uniform, and dressing it up by a receipt to a particular standard of flavour and of composition. The result of such a process may be popular or unpopular; good, bad, or indifferent; but it cannot be Whisky, and it ought not to be sold under the name. We have not the slightest desire to restrict the trade in silent spirit, however this spirit may be flavoured; and all we ask is that it should be conducted openly and not under false pretences, to the detriment of an established and genuine industry. With regard to some articles of commerce and of common consumption, this principle is already affirmed by the existing Adulteration Acts; as, for example, in the permission to sell coffee and chicory under the name of a mixture, although it cannot be sold under the name of coffee without subjecting the vendor to a penalty. The essence of adulteration is not in the character of the thing sold, but in the false representation of its character, or in the substitution of another and a different article for that which is asked for by the buyer and is professedly supplied by the seller. It is quite immaterial to urge that the substituted article is "pure" of its own kind, whatever that may be; and it is manifest that the only object of the false pretence must be to obtain a higher price for what is essentially not only a different but also an inferior commodity. Spirit dealers are not, as a rule, so short-sighted a race as to carry over silent spirit from Scotland or England to Ireland, and to bring it back again, for the mere pleasure of doing so; and we are therefore driven to the conclusion that their customary action in this way is intended to be deceptive, and is, by so far, in its essence fraudulent and nefarious.

CHAPTER VII.

THE ACTION OF THE CHANCELLOR OF THE EXCHEQUER AND OF PARLIAMENT.

IN approaching the part of the question which now opens to us, we leave the debatable ground of opinion, and reach the sure foothold of history.

On the 26th of June, 1874, Mr. O'Sullivan rose in the House of Commons, pursuant to notice—

To call attention to the system which prevails in Her Majesty's bonding stores, in Ireland, of allowing a cheap spirit imported from Scotland to be mixed in those stores with Irish whisky, and re-shipped direct from thence to this country, under bond, which leads the purchaser to believe he is buying Irish manufactured whisky—a practice calculated to injure the character of the Irish spirit trade. The honorable member denounced this system as one calculated to lower the high character which Irish whisky enjoyed in the markets of the world; and one, moreover, which was not creditable to a commercial community. The conduct of the Government in allowing an inferior Scotch spirit to be sold as genuine Irish whisky was as bad as that of the people who painted sparrows and then sold them as canaries. Nay, it was worse, inasmuch as this "silent whisky," as it was termed, sent many a man to his silent grave.

The Chancellor of the Exchequer assured the hon. member—

That the subject had been treated with that consideration which was due to its real importance. Indeed, orders had been sent out in the present week which would, to a great extent, meet the difficulty he had touched upon; but it was impossible for the Government absolutely to guarantee the quality of articles which passed through its hands. All they could do was to make it secure that everything should be sent out with a true name and a true description, and they undertook that spirits which left bonded warehouses should go out with the true mark, showing their real quality. More than that, it was impossible for the Government to do; but the hon. member might rest assured that the utmost attention would be given to the subject.

We take the foregoing report from *Ridley's Wine and Spirit Trade Circular*, in which the question and answer were made the subject of editorial comment, and we must for a moment break the thread of our narrative in order to show that this comment was entirely inaccurate and misleading. It is unnecessary to quote the words, but the substance of them was to deal with the facts as a question between Scotch and Irish Whisky, and to ignore that it was really between Irish Whisky and Scotch silent spirit. The *Circular* gently condemned, or, rather, if we may coin a phrase for the occasion, praised with faint censure, the practice of passing off Scotch Whisky for Irish, but urged that both these spirits were equally unwholesome when new, and equally "the best form of alcohol" when old. The owners of the *Circular* cannot be so ignorant of the rudiments of their professed business as not to know that silent spirit is as wholesome when it is new as at any other period of its—generally very brief—existence. It was never contended that Scotch *Whisky* was unwholesome, for the only essential difference between Scotch and Irish Whisky is a difference of flavour, and, therefore, as regards the consumer, a difference of taste. The cunning device of talking about *Scotch Whisky* has been a very favourite trick with the adulterators and their allies; but we hope we have made it clear, once for all, that Scotch Whisky has really no concern whatever with the question.

To return from this digression to the reply of the Chancellor of the Exchequer, we must call attention to its amazing disingenuousness. Of course, everybody knows that the right hon. gentleman would not have been disingenuous knowingly and of set purpose; but on such a question as this, and on too many more, Cabinet Ministers are the mere puppets of a class of permanent officials, who write down for them what is to be said in reply to departmental questions, and who often, as in this case, put into their mouths the most egregious nonsense. The question was not one of " quality," but one of " genuineness "—a totally different thing from quality, and one which the Government, with the keys of the warehouses in its hand, both is, and ought to be, perfectly well able to guarantee. Nobody would ask the Government to certify that a given sample of Irish Whisky was either good or bad; but they may fairly and properly be asked to certify that they have had the custody of it, and that it is Irish Whisky of some kind. The burden of complaint is, that they allow it to be adulterated in Ireland with foreign admixtures, or even to be altogether a foreign and imported product, and yet to go out again as Irish, this being the interpretation naturally put by purchasers upon a Custom House permit from an Irish port of shipment. The orders said to have been given during the past week—that is, after Mr. O'Sullivan had given notice of his question, and the true mark which is to show real quality, both refer to the same thing—namely, to a Customs regulation that a cask of adulterated spirit shall have the word " blended " marked upon it in letters of a stated magnitude. It must be remembered, however, that this word is not intended to be for the guidance of the buyer or of the seller, but solely for that of the Excise officer. Nevertheless, if the regulation were *bonâ fide* carried out, as it is said to be, it would to some small extent be a protection to the purchaser, who, when he read the word " blended " would naturally ask what were the ingredients of the mixture ? We have constantly urged that the word " blended " should be affixed to every cask of mixed spirit in such a way as to be conspicuous, legible, and not easily effaced ; but what is permitted and done, is to cut the word upon the cask in letters of the specified length, but very slender and shallow. The inscription, as it is thus made, is filled with mud and obliterated by the short and simple process of rolling the cask from the warehouse door to the waggon which takes it away for shipment ; and, by the time the cask reaches its destination, no one could discover the mark except as the result of careful instruction how and where to look for it. The whole answer was merely intended to throw dust into the eyes of the members of the House of Commons, who, of course, had little knowledge of the matter at issue, and who would easily be persuaded by the patient and ever-suffering accents of the Chancellor, that an Irish member had unearthed a sentimental grievance, and was receiving much more notice than either he or it deserved. It need hardly be said that the great official attention given to the subject failed to effect any beneficial changes in the state of things which was complained of, and hence the only possible course was to await the next opportunity of complaining again.

On the 10th of April, 1875, in a debate on the adulteration of Food and Drugs' Bill, Mr. O'Sullivan rose again to propose an amendment:

The object of which was to prevent the sale of a compound known as " Silent Whisky." He had asked a friend of his to try the liquor without letting him know what it was. (A laugh.) His friend drank it, and seeing he made a wry face, he asked him what he thought of it? His answer was, "It was like a torchlight procession going down my throat." (Laughter.) By adulterating with rubbish which was bought at 2s. 8d. per gallon, of course the genuine article which was worth 6s. a gallon, could be undersold. And the Government encouraged that practice, which was so injurious to the health and the sanity of the people. In the Government Stores there were sometimes large quantities of so-called Dublin Whisky, which contained only a very infinitesimal percentage of the genuine article, or even none at all. The Government gave the same permit for the sending out of that poisonous and deleterious stuff as for genuine Whisky, and thus the purchaser and the consumer were deceived and defrauded. The only object of that could be to destroy a branch of Irish industry. ("No," and laughter.) That was no laughing matter. The Irish woollen trade has been destroyed by an Act of Parliament; but in the present case the same thing was being done by more subtle means, namely, by a fraud on the public. He declared he should persevere until the injustice of which he complained was removed.

Mr. O'Sullivan was supported by Mr. Brooks. But the Chancellor of the Exchequer remarked that the subject was one which went far beyond the scope of the Bill then before the House; and he invited Mr. O'Sullivan to a private conference with himself, and with the practical officers of Customs, with a view to the redress of his grievance. This offer was accepted, and the amendment withdrawn. Another year passed away without producing any change in the conditions, and it became manifest that nothing was to be expected from the Government or from the Board of Customs, except as a result of continued pressure.

Accordingly, on the 5th of April, 1876, Mr. O'Sullivan returned once more to the charge—

He rose to call the attention of the House of Commons to the practice which is sanctioned by Her Majesty's Government of blending, and thereby adulterating, Irish Whisky in Her Majesty's

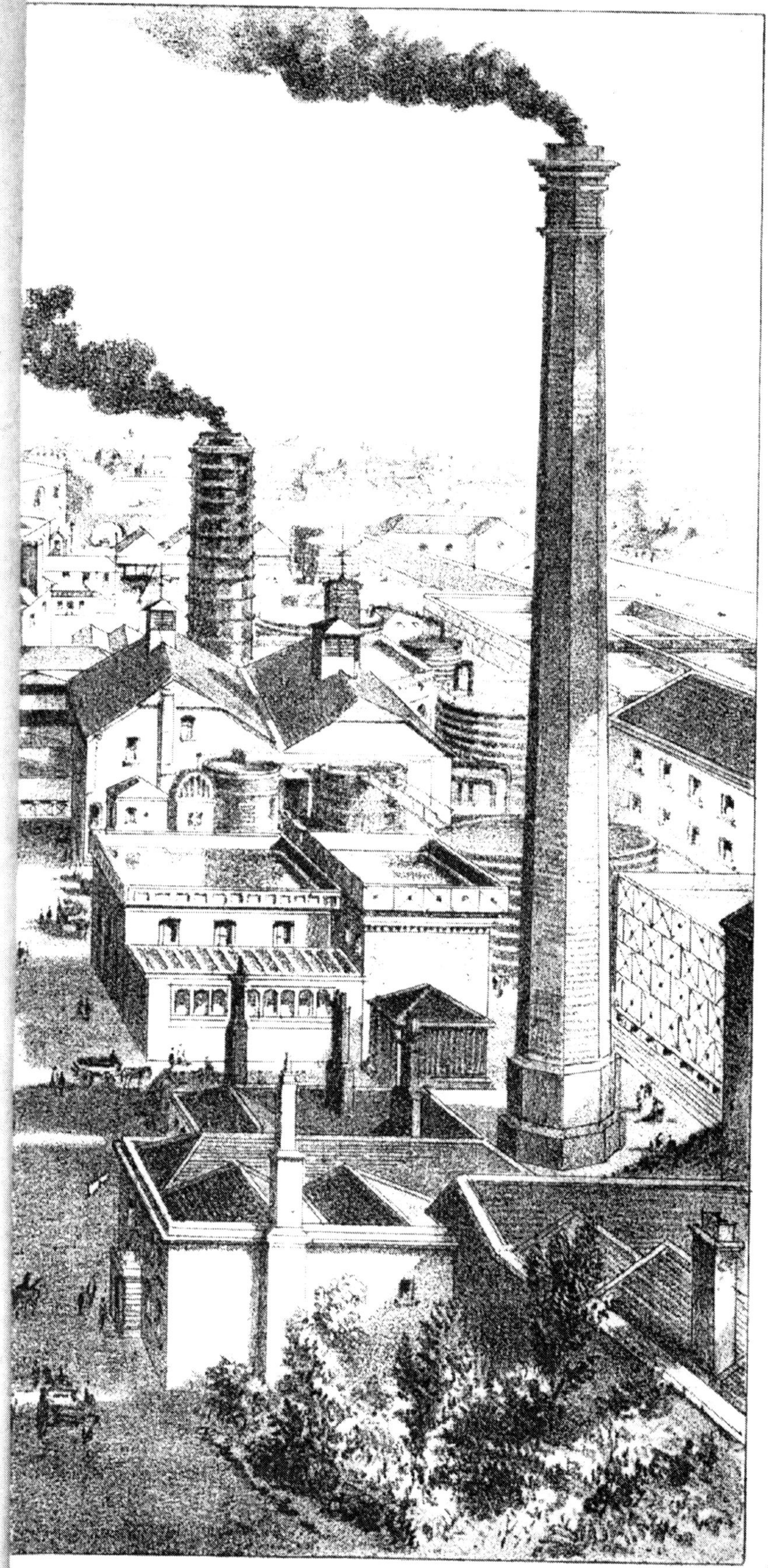

STREET, DUBLIN

Queen Victoria St. E.C.

Customs and Inland Revenue Stores, and to move that a Select Committee be appointed to inquire into the practice. He had first called attention to the subject in June, 1874, when he asked the Chancellor of the Exchequer whether spirits imported into Ireland were allowed to be mixed in the Customs and Inland Revenue Stores and then sent out to the public as pure Irish Whisky, and, if so, whether he would take measures to prevent the continuance of the practice. The Chancellor of the Exchequer replied that it was legal to mix spirits brought from one part of the kingdom to another in the manner described, and that there was no desire on the part of the officers of Inland Revenue that the practice should be discontinued. There had been 122 petitions, signed by 1989 merchants and retailers of spirits in Ireland, praying that a stop might be put to the practice. No inconvenience whatever would arise to legitimate traders from a discontinuance of the practice. He believed that the Chancellor of the Exchequer was inclined to do justice to Ireland in this matter, but he was overruled by the heads of Somerset House, from whom had emanated a celebrated report on the subject. One of the Dublin blenders had written a letter to the Chancellor of the Exchequer, thanking him for not complying with the request, and stating that the English people were fond of cheap Whisky—(a laugh)—and that the blend was sanctioned by Act of Parliament. The " blend " was 2s. cheaper a gallon than pure Irish Whisky, but he wished to show how the public were imposed on by the blenders. He read an advertisement from the blender, who wrote the letter to the Chancellor of the Exchequer, in which the "blend" was described as "bottled under the immediate supervision of the officers of Her Majesty's Customs and Inland Revenue, and, therefore, the public had the absolute guarantee of its being pure Dublin Whisky. (Hear, hear.) Did the Government desire to be considered co-operators in this fraud? In connection with this subject he moved an amendment last Session, but the Chancellor of the Exchequer considered that it was outside the scope of the Bill. The next step was a deputation composed of Irish distillers, who waited on the Chairman of the Board of Customs and his secretary, when the distillers said they would be satisfied if the "blend" were described in the "brand" and in the "permit" as "mixed" Whisky, so that the public might know what they were buying—(hear, hear)—for the Government sent out the same "permit" with the mixed Whisky as with the " pure " Irish Whisky. Shortly afterwards he observed that a deputation of Scotch distillers had waited on the Chancellor of the Exchequer, who were introduced by the member for Glasgow (Mr. Anderson). That hon. gentlemen was reported to have made a most extraordinary statement. He had said the Government had only one duty ; it was a fiscal one—to collect the revenue. (Hear, hear.) Did the hon. gentleman mean to say that the Government owed no moral obligation to the community, to protect the lives, health, and sanity of the public? They might then allow vitriol, bluestone, and any other deleterious material to be sent into the market. They were all aware that Scotland was celebrated for its herrings—(a laugh)— but Scotchmen had discovered how important it was that their herring barrels should be branded. How inconsistent, then, was it for Scotchmen to object to branding Irish Whisky. The *Times* had fallen into a slight error when it asserted that good Irish Whisky was not made in any other town than Dublin. There were several other towns in which good Whisky was made. The fraudulent practice of mixing Whisky was almost unknown in Cork. In an article defending the practice complained of, the *Scotsman* had said that most of the distillers in Ireland were Scotchmen, and that it was simply a matter of Scotch- men outwitting Scotchmen. (Laughter.) He was not aware that there were more than one or two Scotchmen engaged in this particular branch of the trade, but, admitting that all were Scotch- men, that was no reason why the trade itself should be injured by the practice. It was further said that if a fraud was committed it was committed on Irishmen who drank this Whisky. The writer might be a good judge of Scotch toddy, but he knew very little about an Irishman's opinion of Whisky. It was stated in the same article that no Whisky was sold in Scotland as Irish, and it would be impossible to sell any under that name ; but he was able to quote an advertisement extolling the qualities of fine old Irish Whisky, and it was issued from a place no nearer Ireland than Cameron Bridge. (Laughter.) It reminded him of a few enterprising gentlemen in the city who announced that they were making Champagne far superior to that which came from the Champagne country. In a short time they were taken up and prosecuted, but the mixing of Irish Whisky was going on still. In a report upon this subject issued from Somerset House, the excuse offered for a considerable blending of Scotch and Irish spirits was that certain Scotch distillers made a colourless and flavourless spirit which was well adapted for mixing with other spirituous liquors, and it was presumed that it made a palatable compound, or it would not do for dealers to encourage it. It was not stated that this palatable compound was 2s. a gallon cheaper than pure Irish Whisky, but it was stated that the Irish Whisky had the flavour of fusel oil, from which the imported Scotch Whisky was free. In saying that, did not the authorities of Somerset House go out of their way to traduce the Irish product and puff Scotch spirits? The author of the report had made statements which he had in vain been challenged to sustain. He was challenged to test 100 casks of Irish Whisky, not to drink them, but to analyse them, in order to see whether any one contained fusel oil, and he shrank from the contest. It gave the revenue officers a large amount of trouble to watch these mixing operations; and, if they were forbidden, the work of the department would be considerably diminished. He complained that the Government allowed a man who blended spirits to erect in the Custom House Stores a large adulterating shop in the shape of a vat capable of holding 10,000 gallons of Whisky, to bring in an inferior spirit, and, in the presence of Her Majesty's officers, to mix the pure and impure Whiskies, and to send out as pure Irish Whisky the stuff that was filling lunatic asylums and sending men to untimely graves. It was a shame that the State should be a party to the practice, and particularly as it gained nothing by it, for the State got the same duty on pure Whisky that it got on this mixed Whisky. To illustrate the extent to which mixing was carried on, he quoted returns of the contents of certain casks. In the Dublin Custom House a cask of 6,974 gallons contained 4,610 gallons of silent spirit and 2,184 gallons of Irish Whisky. Another cask of 8,206 gallons contained only 299 gallons of Irish Whisky. At Belfast a cask of 5,115 gallons contained only 534 gallons of Irish Whisky; and a cask of 6,417 gallons contained only 1,229 gallons of Irish Whisky. The Scotch spirit could be bought at from 2s. 7d. to 3s. a gallon; and Irish Whisky was worth from 4s. 2d. to 7s. 6d. a gallon. Previous to the Union this tampering with Irish Whisky was unknown; and there were several Acts of Parliament imposing heavy penalties upon any who practised it. It had even been provided at one time that any cask which had been partially emptied should not be filled up at all with the same kind of spirit. By a short clause in an Act of 1860, the existing safeguards were swept away, and he believed that clause could be traced to the same hand as that which penned the report from Somerset House in defence of the silent spirit. He could not see that the Government could have had any other object than to destroy this branch of trade in Ireland. They had increased the duty on Irish Whisky from 2s. 8d. to 10s., an increase of 7s. 4d. between 1852 and 1860, while the increase in England had been 2s. 2d. a gallon, or a little more than a fourth of the increase in Ireland. Worse than the increase of duty was the encouragement afforded to the sale of an inferior article; while, if they would put a stop to the mixing practice, the good article would be sure to go ahead, for it improved by keeping as much as the bad article deteriorated. In 1858, a special Act was passed to allow the manufacture of spirits from rice, from which the fire-water of the Indians was made; and the distillation from rice was the probable explanation of the falling off in the Malt Duty which puzzled the Chancellor of the Exchequer; for, in 1875, Scotland paid duty on 2,722,790 bushels of malt, and made 16,300,161 gallons of spirits; while Ireland paid duty on 3,226,161 bushels of malt, and yet made only 9,381,546 gallons of Whisky and spirits. The Irish distillation was little more than half the Scotch, and yet Ireland paid duty on 500,000 bushels of malt more than Scotland. Were not the Government offering a premium to the manufacturer to make a low-class article when they assisted him in sending it out under the name of a genuine article. The Government did not allow teas to be mixed in bond; they did not allow the white wines of France to be mixed with the sherries of Spain, or the Tarragona ports to be mixed with the fine wines of Portugal, or the brandies of Bordeaux to be mixed with Cognac brandy. Why, then, should they allow any and every sort of spirits to be mixed with Irish Whisky? He would admit that as good malt Whisky was made in Scotland as in any part of the world. But the Scotch manufacturers ought to allow it to stand on its own merits, and not try to sell it as Irish Whisky. (A laugh, and hear, hear.) What would be said if the Government were to allow deeds which were deposited in the registry office to be tampered with for the purpose of private gain? Yet their conduct in allowing Irish Whisky to be tampered with while in their custody was just as bad. It was the habit of some merchants to get over Scotch Whisky and then re-ship it to England as Irish Whisky. That was not done for the purpose of mixing, but was a fraud upon the consumer, and the way to put a stop to it was to direct that it should be retained in bond until it was twelve months old. It was shipped to Ireland, the Scotch permit was cancelled, and it was then shipped to England to deceive the English consumer. The Scotch would not send their Whisky to Ireland for nothing, or unless there was something to be gained by it. If instead of being immediately transhipped it was kept in bond for twelve months the greatest benefit would be conferred upon society, because the Whisky would get rid of all the fusel oil, and would not drive the people mad as it did at present. The hon. gentle man concluded by moving—" That a Select Committee be appointed to inquire into the practice which has been permitted of late years of mixing Whisky in her Majesty's bonding and inland revenue stores with other spirits ; to report to this House whether the practice is injurious to the public and to the manufacturers of Irish Whisky, and whether, in the opinion of the committee, the practice ought or ought not to be discontinued ; and that the committee be also required to inquire into the effects of using new-made spirits, and to report whether it would be in the interest of the public that the Government should detain all spirits and Whisky in bond until it was at least twelve months old." (Hear.)

It is not necessary for us to quote the debate which ensued upon Mr. O'Sullivan's motion, nor even to give the substance of it; but the speech of the Chancellor of the Exchequer is too important to be omitted. The right hon. gentleman declared that—

After listening carefully to the discussion, he saw no reason for departing from the conclusion which he had already arrived at on the subject. What the Government and the Board of Inland Revenue had to look at in a matter of this kind was simply the pro tection of the revenue ; and, so far as their own convenience was concerned, they would only be too glad if there was no mixing in bond. To restrain that practice, however, would be an interference with trade which the Government did not think advisable. It was perfectly true that the practice of mixing spirits in bond had arisen since the year 1860, but the explanation of that was obvious. Previous to the year 1860, different rates of duty were paid on spirits manufactured in different parts of the kingdom, and if mixing had been allowed under those circumstances the interests of the Revenue would have suffered. When the duties in all parts of the United Kingdom were equalised, however, the fiscal reasons for prohibiting mixing in bond disappeared, and manufacturers were allowed to deal with their spirit as they pleased. The argument in favour of non-interference with the practice of mixing was all the stronger from the fact that the bonded stores were the premises of the manufacturers themselves, and were placed under the Government lock and key simply in order that the interests of the revenue should be protected. As a matter of fact, the Government did interfere with manufacturers to the extent of requiring them to put a distinctive mark on casks of blended Whisky, but it was for the purchaser to assure himself of the quality of the article he was buying. If mixing were not allowed in bond, it would certainly be done afterwards, and the Government would then be powerless to check it. He was told there were many cases in which spirit mischievously adulterated was sold by retailers, but he believed that adulteration was effected, not in the Government stores, but in the hands of the retailers themselves. The principle on which the Government went in this matter was to abstain from interfering with processes of trade, or from attempting to give a character to articles which passed through their hands. To imagine that spirits were pure because they came from a Government warehouse was as absurd as to suppose that the Government guaranteed the soundness of an insurance company because its policies bore a Government stamp. He had considered this subject carefully, with every desire to arrive at a proper conclusion, and he had to say that further than marking blended spirits the Government was not prepared to go. Under these circumstances he thought the appointment of a Committee of Inquiry could lead to no good result.

Five or six other speakers followed, and Mr. O'Sullivan offered to withdraw his motion if the Government would mark the permits of blended Whisky. This being declined, a division was taken, and the motion was lost by 145 votes against 69.

On the 1st of May, 1877, Mr. O'Sullivan returned to the charge; and gave notice on that day month he would call attention to the alleged adulteration of Irish Whisky by the addition to it of Scotch silent spirit, while it was under the control of Her Majesty's Officers of Customs. During this session, however, some of the hon. member's own countrymen pursued a policy which totally deranged the course of public business; and hence Mr. O'Sullivan had no opportunity of carrying out his intention. The arguments of the Chancellor of the Exchequer in 1876, such as they were, will be best dealt with in the next chapter, where we shall trace them to their source in the Honble. Commissioners of Customs.

CHAPTER VIII.

THE ACTION OF THE COMMISSIONERS OF INLAND REVENUE.

WE have already intimated that the action of the
Government, in any matter embracing special knowledge, is not so much to be looked upon as that of the
Minister who speaks, as of the irresponsible permanent
officers who coach him, and of whom he is the mouth-
piece. In this matter of Whisky, the voice that uttered
the words given in the last chapter was indeed the
voice of the Chancellor of the Exchequer, but the spirit
which dictated his utterances was that of the Commissioners of Inland Revenue. These gentlemen, some
time before, had issued a report of which we felt bound
to take some notice, lest we should be supposed to
admit that it was correct; and, in the pamphlet to
which we have more than once made reference, it was
criticised in the following words :—

The Commissioners say that it is the proper function of a Revenue
Department to see that no regulations in restriction of the operations
of trade are enforced by their officers but such as are imperatively
required for the security of the Revenue. Like the Roman Emperor,
Vespasian, they hold that the tribute money does not smell of the
source from which it was obtained. They admit, theoretically, that
it might be their duty to interfere if the consequences of non-interference would be prejudicial to the public health ; but they argue
that this condition is not fulfilled in the case under consideration,
because "the silent spirit is a pure and wholesome liquid ;" and they
add the erroneous statement, that " it is notorious that the Dublin

Whisky owes a great part of its peculiar flavour to the fusel oil which it contains, and from which the silent spirit is nearly free." It has of late years been a recognised principle that entire ignorance of everything relating to ships is an essential qualification for the office of First Lord of the Admiralty; and, in like manner, the Commissioners of Inland Revenue have probably thought it a duty to maintain their own freedom from prejudice by keeping themselves in absolute ignorance of everything relating to spirits. Had they not followed this course, they would have known that the very "purity" of the silent spirit which they extol, renders it unfit, or at least unacceptable, for drinking; and hence that the blending which they call harmless necessitates, as its immediate consequence, the deleterious adulteration by which the flavour of true Whisky is supposed to be in some degree imitated. They would have known, also, that fusel oil disappears from true Whisky before it is fit for use, and gives place to new compounds of a wholesome and pleasant character, precisely as the acidity and harshness of green fruit are converted into sweetness and flavour during the natural process of ripening. They should have spoken, therefore, not of " the fusel oil which it contains," but of that " which it once contained ;" and they should also have avoided the further error of saying that Irish Whisky is added to the Scotch spirit as a colouring agent, because it is really inconceivable that they do not know that all Whisky, or, for the matter of that, all spirit, is originally colourless, and hence that the Irish Whisky has no colour to impart. In their plea that restrictions on blending are not required in the interests of the Revenue there is perhaps some force; but these gentlemen undermine their own position when they admit that they might be called upon to interfere if the public health were at stake.

To this criticism the Commissioners replied in their annual report for 1876. They say :—

The grievances of the Dublin distillers have been discussed, both in Parliament, and in newspapers, and pamphlets, at considerable length. We are sorry to find that our statements on the subject have given offence to these gentlemen, but after a careful review of all that we have said or done in the matter we find nothing to retract.

We shall not be led into the indiscretion of joining issue with Messrs. Jameson on the question of our alleged ignorance of the composition of British spirits, nor is it at all necessary for the defence of the position which we have taken up, that we should controvert their doctrine that no spirit made in patent stills is entitled to the name of Whisky. In the Revenue Acts the term does not appear. The spirits made in Scotland, as well as those made in Ireland, are known to us as plain British spirits, and we have no right to make any distinction between them.

We may, perhaps, be allowed to state, as briefly as possible, what the question is, so far as we are concerned, in this matter of mixing Scotch with Irish spirits.

The warehousing of spirits free of duty under the lock of the Revenue officer, is a privilege given to the distillers. They defer payment of the duty on condition that they leave their spirits in our custody. Even in this, its simplest and primary form, the warehousing system was both troublesome and expensive to the Revenue ; and it became much more so, when, for the convenience of the trade, permission was given to carry on within the warehouse many of the operations necessary before bringing the spirits into the market for consumption. It is thus that for their own purposes, and most certainly not in accordance with any interest of Excise and Customs, the proprietors of spirit are allowed to prepare their goods before delivery from warehouse, to suit the tastes and purses of their customers, by mixing the contents of casks of different qualities and ages. They are also allowed to sell their spirits while in bond, and it is the practice to sell them to dealers, the intermediate agents between the distillers and the retailers. Having thus parted with their ownership, and having surrendered all control over it, the Dublin distillers loudly complain that the dealers, before they come to sell the spirits in their turn, find it necessary, or profitable, or desirable, to mix the produce of the Dublin stills with other spirits, chiefly with those made in the patent stills which are in general use in Scotland.

It is in these circumstances that the distillers in Dublin call upon the officers of the revenue to interfere, and to impede or prevent the operations of the dealers which we have described, and they consider themselves deeply aggrieved by the refusal of the Government to take any action whatever.

We must own that we have always felt some difficulty in answering the applications on this subject, but our difficulty is in finding out what there is to answer. We presume that every one will admit that our interference with the operations of trades subject to the excise laws should be strictly limited to such regulations as are necessary for the due collection of the revenues. But if so, why should we be called upon to prescribe to the dealers the nature and quality of the spirits which they may mix? So far as the excise is concerned, nothing could be more desirable than a law prohibiting all mixing or any other operation in bond; it would save us much trouble and expense, incurred solely for the benefit of the traders. But the Dublin distillers are well aware that no Government could now propose to prohibit all manipulation of spirits in bond, and they will not venture to submit to Parliament, as they are quite free to do, an Act for preventing the trade affecting that particular substitution of Scotch for Irish spirits which they complain of. It is rather hard upon us to require, that for their purposes alone—and certainly not for ours—we should make a regulation so opposed to the general convenience of the spirit trade that it is not considered expedient by those who wish for it to propose it to Parliament.

Into the discussion of the merits or demerits of the spirit produced by this mixture we do not enter. We have given some offence by stating in a report to your lordships, which was published, that the Scotch spirits were not impure spirits, and that they contained less fusel oil than the Irish spirits. The remark was made not in order to depreciate the Irish spirits, but as a necessary part of our argument against interference, and in an answer to an allegation that we were bound to prevent the use of an impure and deleterious beverage. But we are quite willing to admit that the spirits produced by the Dublin distillers are among *the finest in the world*, of their kind, and that by the system of bonding for very long periods the effect of the by-product which exists in the new spirit is neutralised.

To these observations we felt bound to offer a reply, and for this purpose we addressed the following letter to the Commissioners :—

HONOURABLE SIRS,

Our attention has been called to certain passages in your recently issued nineteenth report, passages in which you refer to the

G

grievances of us the Dublin distillers, and assert that in your former statements about these grievances you find nothing to alter or to retract. You then proceed to argue the question at some length ; and you do so upon the basis of the assumption, which you think " every one will admit," that " your interference with the operations of trades subject to the Excise laws should be strictly limited to such regulations as are necessary for the due collection of the public Revenue."

It appears to us that in this assumption you not only beg the main question which is at issue, but that you also fail to describe your own practice either accurately or fairly ; and we cannot allow the statements which you have put forth to pass unchallenged. It is due to our own reputation that we should not be regarded as having given even a tacit assent to them.

As regards the general principle, we believe it will be admitted, perhaps even by " everyone," that no body of official persons can rightly allow their conduct to be guided by any rule so simple as that which you have laid down. In a public, as in a private capacity, it is incumbent upon all men to pay some heed to the collateral consequences of their actions, and it is conceivable that you may even be bound, at least by a moral obligation, to sacrifice departmental convenience in order to avoid the infliction of injury upon others. A course of action which would be improper in a private citizen must be at least equally improper in those who are charged with the administration of a department of the State ; and, if so, we hold that you should consider, not merely the collection of the revenue, but also whether your arrangements, however well they may be calculated to facilitate that process, do not also facilitate the practice of fraud. It is, no doubt, true, as a general proposition, that every householder has a perfect right to leave the doors upon his premises open at all hours ; but in any particular case, if it were found that the exercise of this right, although it might be convenient to the possessor, and might even save trouble in his business, had the incidental effect of affording a perpetual free passage to thieves who preyed upon his neighbours, there can be no doubt that such exercise would be prevented, or at least condemned, by public opinion. The case thus supposed is strictly analogous to your actual conduct in the matter now under discussion. For your own convenience, and in direct opposition to the known facts of the case, you assume that all plain British spirits are identical, and you keep yourselves officially ignorant of the very meaning of the word "Whisky." Your assumption of identity and your profession of ignorance together form the open door through which thieves gain access to our premises ; and we contend that you, by whom this door is opened, are morally bound to take care that it is not employed by dishonest persons to our disadvantage. You really concede to us the whole principle by your regulation that vessels which contain blended spirits must be so marked ; but you take away all practical value from this concession, by permitting the marking to be not only inconspicuous, but even illegible. It is perfectly well known that the so-called "blender" has no real *bonâ fide* desire to mix different samples of spirits ; but that his chief, or even his sole object, is to sell silent spirit under the name of Whisky, and to do this by means of a Dublin permit, which has no other use than to deceive the purchaser with regard to the commodity which he buys, and thus to obtain for it a price in excess of that which it would command if its nature were made known. To this deceit you are practically accessories, because, although you know, in the first place, that it is carried on upon a gigantic scale, and, in the second place, that it is only practicable in consequence of your regulations, you still object to modify these regulations in the simple manner suggested by us, which while it would place no impediment in the way of your officers, would, at the same time, render the fraudulent substitution of one kind of spirit for another difficult, if not impossible. Knowing that the Dublin permit has really no meaning at all, you may feel surprise that anybody should be deceived by it ; but the best evidence of its efficacy in this direction is that dealers find it worth their while to pay heavy freights for the conveyance of silent spirit from England and Scotland to Ireland, and *back again*, for no other reason than that this permit may be obtained. It is, unfortunately, the fact that consumers are still so little imbued with the principles which you lay down, that many of them regard a Government permit as something containing statements which may safely be relied upon ; and hence, when they see that a cask has come to them direct from Dublin, it is hard to make them believe that not a single drop of the contained spirit was produced there. Of course, it is possible that in time the public may become educated to the knowledge that assertions made by Custom House authority are only to be looked upon as a series of pleasant fictions ; but before this time arrives it is more than probable that the popularity of the genuine manufacture will have been seriously diminished by the badness of the counterfeits which are palmed off upon consumers under the shadow of your authority.

As regards suggested remedies, we have nothing to add to what we have said on several former occasions. We have always been of opinion that nothing short of the total prohibition of blending in bond will put a stop, either to the fraudulent practices of which we have so much reason to complain, or to others, now well known, by which the State is robbed of many thousands of pounds; and we have urged, and shall continue to urge, pending the total prohibition which we desire, that all permits which are issued by the Government should tell the truth, the whole truth, and nothing but truth, about the liquids to which they severally relate.

In further reference to your main argument, we must beg leave to remind you that you have conceded in an earlier period of the controversy that you could not properly permit poisoning; and, as a matter of official duty, we fail to see the distinction, except in degree, between permitting poisoning and permitting fraud. We can, however, readily understand official objections to take trouble, until this trouble is imposed as a duty either by legislation or by public opinion; and, in the meanwhile, we hail with pleasure the appearance of arguments which not only invite refutation, but which can have no other effect than to hasten the arrival of the reforms which we have so long advocated.

We have the honour to be, Honourable Sirs,
Your most obedient Servants,

(Signed)   WILLIAM JAMESON & CO.   GEORGE ROE & CO.
JOHN POWER & SON.   JOHN JAMESON & SON.

We have reproduced the foregoing letter, because we think it really leaves very little to be said about the main portion of the argument. Privileges, of whatever kind, are given by governments only in order that they may be exercised for legitimate purposes, among which we should be the first to recognise the blending of Whisky, if there were any *bonâ fide* desire to do so for the sake of improving it, or any proper object to be gained by the proceeding. But when our critics know, as well as we know ourselves, that there is no such *bonâ fide* desire or proper object, and that the mixing in bond is done solely for the purpose of deceiving purchasers, then we say that the privilege is one which is abused so grossly that it ought to be withdrawn. In granting the original permission, Government perhaps could not, and we may at least feel sure they did not, foresee the ends to which it would soon be rendered subservient; and, now that these have been shown by experience, the Government ought either to withdraw the privilege or to place proper restrictions upon its exercise. It is a common thing to see it stated, upon letters of recommendation to hospitals and other charities, that the governors hope no attention will be paid to these documents if they are used for begging purposes. Would it not be possible for the Government to take a hint from this practice, and to print across their permits, boldly and legibly and in red ink, that no importance could be attached to anything contained in the document, if it were used as a means of showing in what country the spirit to which it referred had been produced? Experience teaches that hospital letters are used by professional beggars as evidences of poverty, and teaches also that the public would be liable to be misled by them unless the caution was stamped upon the face of each. In like manner, experience teaches—and no one knows this better than the Commissioners of Customs who try to ignore the fact—that Dublin permits are used every day to produce the belief that Scotch silent spirit is Irish, or even Dublin Whisky; and it teaches farther that, notwithstanding Parliamentary disclaimers and official repudiation, the public will be deceived in this manner so long as the permits are issued in their present form. Why should not the remedy, which is known to be moderately effectual in the one case, be applied also in the other? And, when we see that it is not applied, and that no difficulty or obstacle of any kind is placed in the way of an open and notorious fraud, can we arrive at any other conclusion than that the Government does not really desire to stop the practice of deceiving purchasers by means of Excise and Customs documents? We shall see hereafter that, when the revenue suffers, a fraud is checked as soon as it is discovered; but when only private persons suffer, and when the defrauders represent a powerful and a vote-influencing class, official morality goes by on tiptoe, with its eyes half shut, and affects to see nothing but the necessity for an unrestricted trade. So long as the word "trade" is rightly used, we fully agree with the proposition; but we fail to see either the necessity or the advantage of unrestricted lying and cheating. It was not by such means that the commerce of England was created; and adulteration and deception have been by far the most potent agents by which some small portion of it has been destroyed. We have previously pointed out that the so-called argument of the Chancellor of the Exchequer, in the House of Commons, was nothing but a repetition of the lesson which had been taught him by the Commissioners of Customs; and of this, again, their report is nothing more than a somewhat tedious expansion. We do not feel that it requires any more complete refutation of its main argument than that which is contained in our letter and in the immediately foregoing observations.

CHAPTER IX.

RACKING IN BOND—THE GROGGING QUESTION.

WE are now about to see the Commissioners of Customs under a totally new aspect, and to find them sternly repressing a trade freedom which interferes with their own powers and privileges instead of with those of other people. In the spring of last year the following letter was printed as a circular:—

58, North Street, Belfast,
6th March, 1877.

To the Right Hon. and Hon. the Members of the House of Commons.

MY LORDS AND GENTLEMEN,—In your capacity as guardians of the public purse, I beg leave to bring under your notice a leak in the revenue which exists at this port.

The amount I do not know, of course, but I take it to be several times the amount of the cost of the vice-regal establishment in Dublin. £300 per week is supposed to be about the amount of profit realised from it by one firm alone.

The *modus operandi* is this—and I acknowledge that in self-defence I have been compelled to become a participator in the matter. A dealer, or distiller, fills ten puncheons of Whisky, or a hundred, or a thousand, and in the course of a few days the staves of the casks drink up about one gallon and a half of proof spirit each, the duty on which amounts to fifteen shillings on each cask.

The dealer then sends a thousand empty puncheons to the bonded warehouse, and pumps into them the thousand puncheons of Whisky. These second thousand casks proceed to suck up each another gallon and a half of Whisky; and the operator, in the meanwhile, brings

88

home the first thousand casks, pours into each of them a few gallons of boiling water (steam is better, and is used by the more scientific operators), and extracts the gallon and a half of Whisky free of duty. The strength of this spirit is then brought up by the addition of 65 over-proof spirit, and the amount of duty " saved " here is £750 on this one operation, and this is repeated *ad infinitum.*

I have myself " blended " (this operation is called " blending ") Whisky down from 124 over proof to 109 over proof, thereby clearing £9 per puncheon, at the expense of the general tax-payers of the community ; and to stop this, all that is requisite is an order that Whisky shall be blended only once in the bonded stores.

I have the honour to be,

My Lords and Gentlemen,

Your most obedient servant,

(Signed)   J. Torbitt.

The practice described in the foregoing letter, although well known to many persons in the trade, and commonly spoken of under the name of " grogging," was probably wholly unknown to the Commissioners of Customs and to their officers, and its disclosure startled them not a little. Soon after the publication of the letter, on the 1st of May, 1877, Mr. O'Sullivan asked the Chancellor of the Exchequer whether it was a fact that in one warehouse alone (where the Inland Revenue Commissioners admitted the Revenue was defrauded of not less than £13,000) from 400 to 500 casks of Whisky were racked daily, from each of which casks nearly two gallons of proof spirits had been obtained without payment of duty; and whether this evasion of duty had not amounted to over £80,000 per annum in one warehouse alone.

The Chancellor replied as follows :—

The Hon. Member is not correct in his calculation as to the amount of loss that has been sustained by the Inland Revenue from the cause to which he refers. The fact is that in the warehouse in question the number of casks racked do not exceed 420 a week, while the average quantity that could be extracted from each cask did not exceed one and a quarter gallons. The loss to the Inland Revenue therefore only amounted to some £13,000 per annum, instead of £80,000, as stated by the Hon. Member. I may add that, as I stated the other day, the moment the attention of the Inland Revenue Board was drawn to the circumstances they issued instructions that would put a stop to the proceeding.

It may, perhaps, be worth while to pursue this subject a little farther, and to give a succinct history of one of these operations. A dealer, one of the same honest persons who are accustomed, with the approval of the Customs' authorities, to import Scotch spirit into Ireland, that it may be returned as Irish Whisky, brought into a bonded warehouse ninety small casks of spirit, containing as under :—

> 20 casks, 351·5 proof gallons, from Toker, 7th May, 1877.
> 30 casks, 881·6 proof gallons, from Derry, 11th May, 1877.
> 20 casks, 346·5 proof gallons, from Glasgow, May 10th, 1877.
> 20 casks, 338·2 proof gallons, from Glasgow, May 11th, 1877.
> In all, 90 casks, containing 1917·8 proof gallons.

Upon these ninety casks a loss before blending of 35·8 gallons would be allowed, reducing the total to 1882 gallons, and calculated upon a basis of an allowance of 1 per cent. for loss in transit, and 1 per cent. for loss in warehouse before blending; and nearly the whole of this allowance would be for recoverable soakage into the wood.

From each of the ninety casks a sample of three gills was allowed by the regulations to be taken free of duty, which samples would amount to nearly nine gallons in the aggregate; and each cask would absorb into its wood about a gallon and a half of spirit to be afterwards extracted, in all 135 gallons, or, with the samples,

144 gallons, at 64 overproof.   After the lapse of a few days, by an operation called "racking," the ninety casks were emptied into nine large ones, and the emptied casks were taken away to be exhausted of their spirit at the place of business of the dealer.

In order to conceal from the Revenue Officers the large amount of Whisky which the ninety emptied casks would take away with them, a very ingenious device was practised.   In the Customs, the contents of a cask are estimated by a sort of cubic measurement, and the enlargement of the cask at the central part, technically called the "Bulge," is approximately calculated from certain data.   The casks actually constructed for dealers are made to deviate from the standard curvature in two opposite directions; so that they may appear to contain in the bulge either more or less than their actual contents.   The ninety small casks would each hold a little more than they appeared to do by measurement; the nine large ones would each hold a good deal less than they appeared to do by measurement.   So, on the 17th May, when the spirit in the example quoted was estimated, after being transferred to the nine large casks, the account appeared to stand as follows :—

Cask.	Full contents.		Strength		Proof gallons.
1. ...	135 gallons, at	... 65	overproof	...	equals 222·7
2. ...	130 ,,	... 64·8	,,	...	,, 214·2
3. ...	134 ,,	... 63·8	,,	...	,, 219·4
4. ...	129 ,,	... 65	,,	...	,, 212·8
5. ...	137 ,,	... 64·1	,,	...	,, 224·8
6. ...	137 ,,	... 64·1	,,	...	,, 224·8
7. ...	182 ,,	... 64·6	,,	...	,, 217·2
8. ...	130 ,,	... 64·4	,,	...	,, 213·7
9. ...	85 ,,	... 64·9	,,	` ...	,, 140·1

Or nine casks, apparently containing 1889·7 proof gallons.

Hence the Revenue Officers would find an apparent increase of 7·7 proof gallons (from 1882 to 1889·7) in the quantity of Whisky; and they would attribute this to the difference between the nine bulges and the ninety, little suspecting that the difference was really, and very greatly, the other way; and that the nine bulges concealed an absolute deficiency of nearly 150 gallons. Of course, the dealer to whom the spirit belonged would not pay duty upon it in the large casks, but would rack it off again, into smaller ones, before taking it out of bond for his customers.

Arrangements of this kind were, of course, a natural outcome of the practice of blending for the purpose of diluting good spirit with that which was worse, but the enormity of the transgression incidentally committed roused the Board of Revenue to an acute sense of their duty which no frauds upon private persons had ever been able to excite. Mr. Torbitt's letter was dated March 6th; and, on the 5th April following, the Board issued the following minute:

The Board having received a communication from the Inland Revenue Department, suggesting that certain regulations recently issued in respect to the racking or blending of British spirits in Excise Warehouses may be adopted in this force with respect to British spirits in Customs Warehouses, viz. :—

British spirits which have been racked or blended in warehouse shall not be re-racked or re-blended, except upon the following conditions, viz. :—

The spirits shall be returned into the same casks, which shall not in the meantime be removed from the warehouse; or they shall be put into smaller casks, none of which shall exceed three-fourths of the capacity of any of the original casks; and on the heads of every cask containing such spirits there shall be painted legibly, by the trader, the word "Re-racked," or "Re-blended," as the case may be.

When the original casks are not used again, the officer must see that they are thoroughly drained before they have removal from the warehouse.

In order to evade this well-meant regulation, the honest dealers who blend Whisky at once proceeded to order a number of large casks, capable of containing from 220 to 160 proof gallons each, so that, while diminishing the size of the new cask at each operation by one-fourth, in accordance with the order, they might yet have seven re-rackings before they came down to the 30 gallon cask. Thus:—

220 gallons, minus one-fourth, equals 165 gallons.

165	,,	,,	,,	,,	124	,,
124	,,	,,	,,	,,	93	,,
93	,,	,,	,,	,,	70	,,
70	,,	,,	,,	,,	53	,,
53	,,	,,	,,	,,	40	,,
40	,,	,,	,,	,,	30	,,

The order about drainage of the casks was of very little consequence, the spirit which they carried away each time not being, as the Board appear to have fancied, loose within their cavities, but having been absorbed into the substance of the staves. By careful draining there would, indeed, be some small loss from evaporation, but the bulk of the abstracted spirit would require hot water or even steam for its complete withdrawal from the wood. The only effectual regulation, if re-racking were still permitted, would be to have the casks steamed upon the warehouse premises, under the supervision of the revenue officers.

After a lapse of four months, the authorities appear to have discovered that the abstraction of spirit by the staves of casks was going on as merrily as ever; and, on the 10th of August, they issued another order, which seems really to have given the practice its *coup de grace*. This new order was as follows :—

In addition to the existing regulations for the racking and
blending of British spirits in warehouse before payment of the
duty thereon, it is further ordered that in future no such spirits
be allowed to be racked or blended more than once except on
the condition that they are returned into the same casks from
which they are taken ; and that such casks are not in the meantime
taken out of the warehouse. Proprietors of spirits are to be
informed, however, that the Board will consider any emergency
requiring the substitution of other casks ; but before assenting
thereto they must be satisfied that the emergency is such as
could not have been provided for when the spirits were first
racked or blended in warehouse.

By a general order of the 11th December, 1877, it is
further ordered " that no objection be made to spirits
already racked being again racked into other casks, if
such casks be *bonâ fide* required for exportation or ship's
stores, and on condition that the spirits be exported
direct from the warehouse in which such racking takes
place."

The last quoted order, that of December 11th, was
manifestly only intended to save the Board the trouble
of considering every case of a class in which it was
clearly proper that the desired permission should be
granted ; and the original or August order has
effectually, for the present at least, extinguished the
lucrative business which we have described. We
have even heard that one dealer has been explaining
to his customers that he can no longer supply them
with the liquid which it pleases him to call " Whisky "
at so cheap a rate as heretofore, since he has " lost "
£6,000 a year by the unforseen termination of his
" grogging " business. Necessity is the mother of
invention, and there can be little doubt that the
schemes of persons of this class will again, before very
long, give trouble to those whose hard task it is to

endeavour to keep them within the paths of rectitude. We feel, however, that the Board of Inland Revenue, whose pleasure it is to allow us to be robbed easily by virtue of its regulations, and which has persistently refused to lift a finger either in our defence or in defence of honest dealing, has no right to be surprised if the spirit of dishonesty which it has cherished should recoil upon its own head. The difference between the official estimate of fraud upon the revenue and of fraud upon us is amusing; and, if the two estimates are inconsistent with each other, the difference is at least not inconsistent with human nature. We cannot but think, however, that our Customs and Excise authorities would find their own battle against dishonesty less arduous if they would strive to banish dishonesty in general, and not only those varieties of it which affect the national income. By permitting the general business of spirit dealing to become saturated with dishonest practices at which they wink, they bring into this business a number of utterly unscrupulous persons who are unaccustomed to nice distinctions, and who, if they see an opportunity of making illicit profit, care nothing whether they do so at the cost of their friends and patrons the Commissioners of Customs, or at the cost of honest traders like ourselves.

We have seen already that the first blow struck at the practice of grogging was struck by the enforcement in the Customs of a regulation which existed previously in the Excise; and we may point out that great opportunities of wrong-doing are afforded by the differences between the rules of the two departments. Not only is this so, but the estimates for duty of the Customs officers are frequently increased by the Excise, when spirits pass from one department to the other; and troublesome surcharges are thus constantly arising. The Customs authorities estimate the contents of a cask by measure only, omitting tenths of a gallon, while the Excise determine the contents exactly, both by weight and measure. An uniformity of system between the two departments would not only be a great boon to distillers and dealers, but it would also take away opportunities for fraud.

CHAPTER X.

WHISKY FRAUDS OUTSIDE THE BONDED WAREHOUSES.

IT has often been said that the horse, although one of the noblest of animals, seems, by a sad fatality, to be the occasion of dishonesty amongst the great majority of those who systematically endeavour to turn him to profitable account; and what is true in this respect of the horse is at least equally true of spurious Whisky. The only point of difference is that the exciting cause of dishonesty in the latter case is itself dishonest; and there can be no question that many of those who habitually buy and sell it will not only make any false pretence with regard to it which they fancy may promote its sale, but they will even, in no small number of cases, incur the risk of coming within the provisions of the criminal law. A very common trick is to sell spurious Whisky in casks bearing the brand and trade mark of one of the authors of this volume; and it is a business in large towns to collect our empty casks from dealers, who obtain for them a larger price than the actual casks would be worth when new, and who sell them on these terms to people who resell them, of course at a profit, to other dealers, who fill them with rubbish of their own manufacture or of their own blending, and then sell this rubbish as if it were of our veritable make and of the date which is borne upon the cask in which it is placed. We have sought in vain for some practically available method of checking this form of deception, for it is quite impossible for us to trace our casks, to insist upon their being returned, or to discover what becomes of them. All we can do is to maintain the permanent offer of a large reward for any person who will enable us to prosecute to conviction any dealer by whom the public has been deceived in the manner set forth.

During the past year, by great good fortune, one of our number has been able to expose a transaction of a somewhat analogous kind, although the element of the original cask was wanting; and the particulars of this case are so instructive that they are worthy of being detailed at length. A Mr. Erwin, who, at that time, was landlord of the Limerick Inn, Great Bridge, Tipton, was in Birmingham on the 24th September, 1875, and he met there a Mr. Williams, a traveller in the employment of Mr. Groome, a wine and spirit merchant at Chester, who carried on business as Groome and Sons. Williams solicited an order, and Mr. Erwin asked him at what price he could supply John Jameson and Son's Whisky. After some bargaining, Williams took an order for three hogsheads at 4s. 6d. a gallon, and a memorandum was made of the transaction. Two days later Mr. Erwin received an invoice from the house at Chester, charging him with three hogsheads of John Jameson and Son's Whisky of 1875, numbered respectively 7096, 7097, and 7098. With the invoice were three documents, purporting to be bond warrants describing the three hogsheads, and saying that they were bonded in the preceding April by John Groome, and that they were held subject to rent from September, 1876. Happy in the supposed possession of his Whisky, Mr. Erwin paid for it in due course, and left it undis-

H

turbed until March, 1877, when he sold the hogshead, No. 7096, to one purchaser, and the other two to another. Mr. Reynolds, the purchaser of the single hogshead, No. 7096, wrote to Groome and Sons, and instructed them to forward it to his order under bond to bonded stores at Birmingham. To this they objected, and offered to pay duty, and send it to him direct, but Mr. Reynolds insisted upon his orders being carried out, and they were forced to do their best to comply. A cask of spirit was sent in the manner directed, and on this cask the name of John Jameson and Son, and the specified number, appeared in freshly-painted letters; but Mr. Reynolds was not satisfied with either the appearance of the cask or the quality and apparent age of the spirit, and inquiries were set on foot. It then turned out, first, that Groome had never possessed the Whisky specified in the invoice, and, secondly, that the cask sent to Mr. Reynolds was Whisky made in 1877 by the Middleton Distillery Company at Cork. John Jameson & Son's hogsheads of 1875, numbered respectively 7096, 7097, and 7098, were not filled until the month of June in that year, and they were sold by the makers to Messrs. Cobbold, of Ipswich, in whose cellars they were still remaining, and untouched, when the delivery to Mr. Reynolds was made by Groome. The firm of Groome & Sons had therefore professed to sell a specific article which they had never possessed, they charged warehouse rent for this article when it was not warehoused, and, being called upon to deliver, they sent new Whisky of another maker, worth not more than half the value that John Jameson & Son's Whisky of 1875 had attained in 1877. Upon these facts being brought to light, Messrs. John Jameson & Son induced Mr. Erwin to allow them to undertake a criminal prosecution against Groome, for obtaining money under false pretences; and the case came before the magistrates at West Bromwich on the 24th of September. The main facts having been proved as above, the further hearing was adjourned for a fortnight. During the intervening time, the prosecution was advised that, in order to establish the criminal charge against Groome, it would be necessary to prove his personal knowledge of and consent to the fraud; and the legal proof for this purpose might not have been forthcoming, however strong might be the presumption. There would have been small satisfaction in convicting a cellarman, or clerk, or other subordinate person; and so the overtures of the defendant for a compromise were favourably considered. Messrs. Jameson & Son consented to withdraw from the prosecution upon the payment by Groome of the sum of £1,200 for costs and damages, and upon receipt of a proper apology, which they were to be at liberty to advertise at their discretion for twelve months after the hearing. It is hardly necessary to say that these terms were at once accepted.

It is tolerably manifest in the history of the above transaction, that the purchaser, Mr. Erwin, had his mind completely set at rest about his purchase by the documents purporting to be bond warrants which he received; and it therefore cannot be too widely known that these documents are in no sense official, but that they are issued by dealers at their own will and pleasure, and have no more real value than a cheque, which may or may not represent assets available to meet it when it is presented. In this instance, for example, the specified assets were not in the bonded warehouse, and never had been there. A somewhat similar deception is often

practised by means of delivery orders to distillers. A
dealer buys Whisky of a distiller, and leaves it in the
distiller's warehouse in bond, paying some small annual
rent for the privilege. In course of time he sells it, and
on receiving the price he gives the purchaser an order
on the distiller for the specified cask of Whisky. When
the transaction is a *bonâ fide* one, this is all as it should
be, but many purchasers put such an order away in a
place of safety, under an impression that it gives them
an indefeasible right to their purchase. They allow
their Whisky, as they fondly consider it, to mature in
bond; and, after the lapse of a few years, they present
the order, only to discover that the cask has long before
been delivered to another purchaser. They do not seem
to reflect that there is nothing in the world to prevent
a dishonest person from selling the same cask of Whisky
to twenty different people, if they are ready to pay for
it and to put away the delivery order without inquiry.
It is as easy to write a delivery order as to write anything else, and the person who receives one should
immediately send it to the distillers, so that he may be
recognised by them as the owner, and the Whisky be
placed at his disposition instead of being left at the disposition of the previous owner. The distiller can do no
more than act upon the first delivery order which is presented to him; and, if a second or a third order for the
same cask is presented subsequently, there is nothing
left for him but to wonder at the credulity of men of
business, who have parted with their money in exchange
for a few written and printed characters upon a piece of
paper, and without any recognition of the validity of
these characters, or even knowledge of their existence,
on the part of those to whom they are addressed.

It will at once be manifest that a large proportion of

the frauds upon dealers and consumers, which these pages have been written to expose, are indebted for their success to an absolute want of knowledge, even among those who might be expected to possess it, of the odour, flavour, and other characters of genuine and well-matured Whisky. For several years past, during which the dealers have stood between the distillers and the consumers, the first-named class have scarcely suffered genuine Whisky to go into the market, so systematically has it been reduced and diluted, and otherwise bedevilled. The stuff sold under the name of Whisky is generally, at least, as inferior to genuine Whisky as the poorest rhubarb wine is to the finest brands of champagne, and could not be made to pass muster for Whisky with any who had once become acquainted with the real spirit. In these circumstances the authors, although they will not in the future, any more than in the past, interfere with the ordinary mode of distribution of their manufacture, have yet thought it a clear duty to provide means for securing that the public may have access to genuine Whisky, may become acquainted with its characters, able to procure it with ease and certainty when it is demanded, and to use it as a standard of quality by which to estimate the worth of spurious imitations. For this purpose, Messrs. W. Jameson & Co., of the Marrowbone Lane Distillery, and Messrs. George Roe & Co., of the Thomas Street Distillery, have determined to bottle from four to six year-old Whisky in bond, and to secure every bottle with a mark and capsule which it will be felony to forge or imitate. The Whisky thus bottled will be supplied to the trade by the usual channels, and may be purchased by the public from any retailer of wines and spirits. Such Whisky would be of guaranteed age, genuineness, and excéllence ; but those who desire the very finest which can possibly be obtained must themselves exercise some foresight, by buying in the wood and keeping in bond until the time when their purchase will no longer improve with age. It may then be bottled and laid aside for use. In such a transaction the purchaser, it need hardly be said, must [not allow himself to be treated after the fashion of Mr. Erwin, but must obtain certainty, by proper inquiries, that what he has bought is what and is where it is represented to be. He should then have the cask delivered at his own house, and bottled there under his personal supervision. We do not wish to imply that honesty is extinct in the world, but it is a fact that spirit dealers would rather, if they could, sell silent spirit than Whisky, if only on the ground that the latter requires no maturation and returns them a larger profit. It is by no means to their interest that genuine Whisky should be readily procurable; because it would not fail to create awkward inquiries with regard to much of the stuff which is sold under the same name ; and, when dealers generally are actively or passively inimical to a given article, the private consumer must take a little trouble if he is determined to possess it. It is said that any one who wishes to bring to Europe an exceptionally fine case of Havannah cigars must be present when the case is packed and closed at the factory, and must then remain in personal contact with it, walking by the side of it when it is being moved, and sitting upon it when it is at rest, until the ship which brings it is not only under weigh, but has even sent back her pilot. The case is not quite so bad as this about the finest Whisky ; but this book has been written to little purpose if our readers

have not discovered that a fair proportion of spirit
dealers are what would be called "smart men" in the
United States; and that those who deal with them, or
buy the commodity in which they are interested, must
not fail, again in Yankee phraseology, to keep their own
eyes well skinned during their transactions. To this
counsel we need only add the assurance that, although
we advise our friends to take trouble to obtain genuine
Whisky, we have not the smallest fear that anyone will
ever complain that the trouble, if actually taken, has
been thrown away, or even that it has been only imper-
fectly rewarded. To most Englishmen, and to many
Scotchmen and Irishmen, the taste of genuine Whisky
will not only be a delightful sensation, but also a new
one; and those to whom it is so will assuredly share
our own indignation at the miserable artifices by which
something totally different has for a long period been
so industriously pushed forward under the name.

JJ & S
TRADE MARK.

JOHN JAMESON & SON,

Bow Street Distillery, Dublin.

TRADE MARK.

WM. JAMESON & CO.,

Marrowbone Lane Distillery, Dublin.

P
TRADE MARK.

JOHN POWER & SON,

John's Lane Distillery, Dublin.

G R
TRADE MARK.

GEORGE ROE & CO.,

Thomas Street Distillery, Dublin.

FAC-SIMILE

OF

LABELS, CAPSULES, AND BRANDS ON CORKS

USED FOR THE

Bottled Whisky

OF

MESSRS. WM. JAMESON & CO.

Marrowbone Distillery,

AND OF

MESSRS. GEO. ROE & CO.,

Thomas Street Distillery,

Fac-Simile of Label issued by Messrs. WM.
JAMESON & CO., printed in Gold and
Black on White Enamel Paper.

Fac-simile of Capsule.
Gilt Foil.

Fac-simile of Brand
on Cork.

CAUTION.—Every Bottle bears the above Label, Capsule, and Brand
on Cork.

*May be had of all respectable Wine and Spirit Merchants, including those named
on following pages.*

WHOLESALE OF

Messrs. TROWER & LAWSON	39, St. Mary-at-Hill, London.
Messrs. GEORGE PIM & CO.	Tithebarn Street, Liverpool.
Messrs. E. YOUNG & CO.	Seel Street, Liverpool.
Messrs. E. S. PICK & CO.	82, Lower Thames Street, London.
Messrs. H. B. FEARON & SON	33, Holborn Viaduct, London.
Messrs. H. B. FEARON & SON	145, New Bond Street, London.
Messrs. J. R. PHILLIPS & CO.	Nelson Street, Bristol.
Messrs. MOORE, VICARS & CO.	Batchelor Street, Liverpool.
Messrs. GARRARD & BARTRAM	43 & 44, Welsh Back, Bristol.
Messrs. J. R. PARKINGTON & CO.	24, Crutched Friars, London.
Messrs. H. BRETT & CO.	26 & 27, High Holborn, London.
Messrs. J. F. BIGGS & CO.	The Arches, Ludgate Hill, London.
Messrs. HUDSON BROTHERS	43, Moorgate Street, London.
Messrs. J. L. PFUNGST & CO.	23, Crutched Friars, London.
Messrs. T. L. WILLIS & CO.	17, Fenchurch Street, London.
Messrs. HUDSON & KENNEDY	11, Queen Victoria Street, London.
Messrs. H. B. FEARON & SON	Dewsbury, Yorkshire.
Messrs. ROBERT JAMES & CO.	17, Store Street, London.
Messrs. STAPLETON & CO.	203, Regent Street, London.
Messrs. J. NIMMO & SON	Castle Eden, Co. Durham.
Messrs. H. MULLENEUX & SON	Dale Street, Liverpool.
Messrs. JORDAN & CO.	Watergate Street, Chester.
Messrs. JORDAN & CO.	61, Jermyn Street, London.
Sir C. CUNNINGHAM & CO.	Old Jewry Chambers, London.
Messrs. BRAYLEY, SELKIRK & CO.	The Grove Bristol.
Messrs. BALL & SKEATES	Little King Street, Bristol.
Messrs. R. W. BELLAMY & CO.	Berkeley Place, Bristol.
Messrs. MOORE, HANSON & CO.	Princess Street, Bristol.
Messrs. MORTIMER & CLUNE	15, Small Street, Bristol.
Messrs. J. NIMMO & SON	87, Clayton Street, Newcastle.
Mr. F. PERKINS	Southampton.
Messrs. J. NIMMO & SON	6, Atherton Street, Liverpool.
Mr. A. T. PERKINS	Southsea.
Mr. WM. POTTER	88, Tower Hill, London.
Messrs. POWELL & MACKENSIE	9, Quay Head, Bristol.
Mr. ADAM HILL	258, High Holborn, London.
BRADDOCK & LARNER	18, Fenchurch Street Buildings, E.C.
Messrs. JOHN HOPE & CO.	Montreal. Agents for the Dominion of Canada.
Messrs. J. SACCONI & CO.	Agent for Gibraltar.
Messrs. TURNER, BEETON & CO.	Victoria. Agents for British Columbia.
Messrs. JAMES REID & CO.	Agents for New York, and the United States of America.

Fac-simile of Label issued by Messrs. GEO. ROE & CO., printed in Black on White Enamel Paper

SECURED BY OUR NAME & BRAND ON THE CAPSULE.
CORK AND LABEL.

Old Malt Whiskey.

Geo. Roe & Co.,

Distillers,

G R
★ ★ ★

Dublin.

BOTTLED IN BOND

Fac-simile of Capsule.
White Foil.

Fac-simile of Brand
on Cork.

CAUTION.—Every Bottle bears the above Label, Capsule, and Brand on Cork.

May be had of all respectable Wine and Spirit Merchants, including those named on following pages.

WHOLESALE OF

Messrs. TROWER & LAWSON	39, St. Mary-at-Hill, London.
Messrs. PORTAL, DINGWALL & CO. ...	2, Idol Lane.
Messrs. R. HOOPER & SONS	29, Queenhithe.
Messrs. BOORD & SON	Bartholomew Close, London.
Messrs. H. BRETT & CO.	High Holborn, London.
Messrs. H. B. FEARON & SON ...	Holborn Viaduct, London.
Messrs. B. M. TABUTEAU & SONS ...	Jermyn Street, London.
Messrs. B. A. MOORE & SON	146, Fleet Street, London.
Messrs. JAS. CONSTABLE & CO. ...	The Exchange, Southwark Street, London.
Messrs. DELMAR BROTHERS	63½, King William Street, London.
Messrs. WILLIAMS, JONES, & LAWS ...	11, Queen Victoria Street, London.
Messrs. A. C. DAVIS	26, Wigmore Street, London.
Messrs. C. J. DOTESIO	19, Swallow Street, Piccadilly, London.
Messrs. E. A. LEVY & CO.	72, Cornhill Street, London.
Messrs. ROBERT SMITH	137, Fenchurch Street, London.
Messrs. THOS. SERCOMBE & SON ...	71, Fleet Street, London.
Messrs. R. J. SAUL & CO.	4, Waterloo Place, Pall Mall, London.
Messrs. CLIFFORD, SMITH & CO. ...	137, Fenchurch Street, London.
Messrs. J. A. PLUMMER...	128, High Street, Clapham, London.
Messrs. BASIL, WILLIS & CO.	Charles Street, Grosvenor Square, London.
Messrs. BOSS BROTHERS	4, Jermyn Street, London.
Messrs. T. W. STAPLETON & CO. ...	203, Regent Street, London.
Messrs. H. E. EARLE & CO.	82, Grosvenor Street, London.
Mr. A. W. FOXWELL	147, Edgware Road, London.
Messrs. PAGE & SANDEMAN	5½, Pall Mall, London.
Messrs. MOREL BROTHERS	210 & 211, Piccadilly, London.
Messrs. D. H. WESTON	24, North End, Croydon.
Messrs. C. GODWIN & CO.	53, High Street, Notting Hill, London.
Messrs. STEPHEN UNWIN	27, Park Street, Regent's Park, London.
Messrs. E. G. JELL	High Street, New Brompton, London.
Messrs. R. PRESTON & CO.	Liverpool.
Messrs. H. MULLENEUX & SONS ...	Liverpool.
Trustees of J. M. THRELFALL... ...	Liverpool.
Messrs. GLAZEBROOK & RIGBY ...	Liverpool.
Messrs. IHLERS & BELL	Liverpool.
Messrs. GEORGE BARKER	Liverpool.
Mr. WILLIAM WINDSOR	Liverpool.
Mr. R. DAWSON	Birmingham.

WHOLESALE OF

Messrs. A. & J. M'CONNELL	Leeds.
Messrs. STEPHENSON, ROUTLEY & CO.	Manchester.
Messrs. EVANS & CO.	Chester.
Messrs. G. P. COLLARD & SON... ...	Canterbury.
Messrs. WALLER & SON	Bradford.
Messrs. J. SPINK & SON	Bradford.
Messrs. W. H. HOLLOWAY	Bradford.
Messrs. J. H. & J. BROOKE	Folkestone.
Messrs. E. W. WOODFORD & SON ...	Gravesend.
Messrs. P. SMITH & SON	Hurstpierpoint.
Mr. G. W. MOORE	Walsall.
Messrs. G. W. MITCHELL	Taunton.
Messrs. GRAVES & GIFFORD	Worcester.
Messrs. PLEWS & SON	Darlington.
Messrs. WILEY & CO.	Sheffield.
Mr. HENRY WILSON	Hull
Mr. F. C. THOMPSON	Hull.
Messrs. JOSEPH WRIGHT & CO. ...	Burton-on-Trent.
Messrs. J. & W. SANT	Stoke-on-Trent.
Mr. D. WATERS	Brighton.
Messrs. E. C. PARSONS & CO.	Brighton.
Mr. R. C. WILKINSON...	Exeter.
Messrs. NARRACOTT & CO.	Plymouth.
Mr. JOHN ELLERY	Plymouth.
Mr. N. ANTILL	Portsmouth.
Mr. E. J. WINDSOR	Liskeard.
Mr. H. F. RAYNES	Ventnor, Isle of Wight.
Messrs. GEORGE COPE & SON	Wolverhampton.
Messrs. GEO. PETERS & CO.	Southsea.
Mr. JOSEPH ARNOLD	St. Leonard's-on-Sea.
Mr. T. OWENS	Banbury.
Messrs. FULTON, DUNLOP & CO. ...	Cardiff.
Messrs. H. B. FEARON & SON ...	Dewsbury, Yorkshire.

LONDON:

PRINTED BY SUTTON SHARPE & CO.,

145, QUEEN VICTORIA STREET, E.C.

CPSIA information can be obtained at www.ICGtesting.com
Printed in the USA
LVOW111943061112

306128LV00018B/218/P